on track ...

Bucks Fizz

every album, every song

David Waterfield

sonicbondpublishing.com

Sonicbond Publishing Limited
www.sonicbondpublishing.co.uk
Email: info@sonicbondpublishing.co.uk

First Published in the United Kingdom 2026
First Published in the United States 2026

British Library Cataloguing in Publication Data:
A Catalogue record for this book is available from the British Library

ISBN 978-1-78952-448-2

Typeset in ITC Garamond & ITC Avant Garde
Printed and bound in England

Graphic design and typesetting: Full Moon Media

Follow us on social media:

Twitter: https://twitter.com/SonicbondP

Instagram: https://www.instagram.com/sonicbondpublishing_/

Facebook: https://www.facebook.com/SonicbondPublishing/

Linktree QR code:

on track ...

Bucks Fizz

every album, every song

David Waterfield

sonicbondpublishing.com

Acknowledgements

Firstly, I would like to thank Stephen Lambe of Sonicbond Publishing for taking a chance on me. I didn't know if anyone would be interested in a book about Bucks Fizz. Thank you for allowing me the opportunity to write one.

I would also like to thank the following.

Colin Simpson, for digging out those Bucks Fizz Fan Club newsletters and for being with me at my first Bucks Fizz concert. Chris Boyce, for his continual support, encouragement and kindness. He is the only person who knew that I was writing this book and was the voice of reason on many occasions when I was pushing myself much too hard.

Nigel Hall, who gave me my first *On Track* book and, in doing so, planted the idea that I could write one, too.

Beth Coey-Archer, Karen Dunn and Scott Leedham for believing in me, even when I don't always believe in myself.

Kirsty Briggs, for giving me the time I needed to write this book and the Rainbow Book Club for bearing with me while I did.

Finally, this book is dedicated to my Mum, Mary Waterfield. We shared that Eurovision night in 1981 together. She was the responsible adult in charge of three excitable teenagers at our first ever Bucks Fizz concert at Birmingham Odeon in 1983 and that was not her only Bucks Fizz concert! She was amazing, beautiful, kind and irreplaceable. I miss her every day.

Foreword

It was Saturday 4 April 1981. The 26th Eurovision Song Contest was being televised live on the BBC from the Simmonscourt Pavilion in Dublin. My Dad, who was never a fan of Eurovision, had escaped to the pub with his Brother-In-Law to avoid it all. However, my Mum and I were avid Eurovision fans, so we were both glued to the television, laughing at the affectionate, dry humour of Terry Wogan and cheering for the UK entry, an attractive and likeable group called Bucks Fizz and their song 'Making Your Mind Up'. In truth, it wasn't my favourite song in the contest, nor was I at all certain that it would win. I had a sneaking feeling that the Swiss entry, 'Io Sensa Te', by Eurovision veterans Peter, Sue and Marc, could steal the victory. My Mum had no such qualms. She was convinced from the outset that Bucks Fizz would win. It was close, and it went right to the final vote, but we were both delighted when she was proved right.

If you mention the name Bucks Fizz to most people, the song that they will probably recall is their Eurovision winner from that night, 'Making Your Mind Up', or possibly 'The Land Of Make Believe'. However, there is so much more to Bucks Fizz than these two songs. As a teenager, I devoured their singles and albums, pictures of the group adorned my bedroom walls and I saw them live at venues from Lancashire to London. I am not being the slightest bit ironic when I say that Bucks Fizz made some of the finest pop music of the 1980s. They were far more eclectic than they were ever given credit for, and their records rarely received the credibility that they deserved. When Tommy Vance stated on BFBS Radio in November 1986, 'I have every album Bucks Fizz have ever made. Most of them, I've got two copies – one copy at home and one in the car – because I think they're some of the finest constructed records ever put together in this country', I not only agreed with him, but I wanted to thank him for saying it.

Being publicly 'out' as a Bucks Fizz fan at school wasn't always a comfortable place to be, but I have never subscribed to the idea that pop music is somehow a lower art form, less deserving of attention than other genres, or a 'guilty pleasure' to be hidden away whilst publicly declaring allegiance to something more credible. I would also repudiate some of the unfair criticism levelled at the group. Bucks Fizz were blessed to have an Ivor Novello Award-winning songwriter at the helm and world-class musicians playing on their records. The group's original material was covered by other artists, including Cher and Agnetha Faltskog, and anyone dismissive of the group's own ability should start with the flawlessly lovely 'Now Those Days Are Gone' and proceed from there.

I guess that leads me to my reasons for writing this book. I have always loved Bucks Fizz. They made some tremendous pop records, and in 2023, I was delighted to have the opportunity to write a review of *The Land Of Make Believe – The Definitive Collection* for a website called Midlands Rocks. I found myself editing my review down, wanting to say much more about the tracks and wishing that there were a book that celebrated the group and their music, so I thought that I would have a go at writing one! My hope is that this book contributes a little to an appreciation of Bucks Fizz and encourages others to explore a body of work that has brought me so much pleasure in my own life. This book is a labour of love, dedicated to the group themselves, and from one Fizz fan to all the others. I hope you will receive and enjoy it in that spirit.

What This Book Is And Is Not

This is not the story of Bucks Fizz. That would require a much bigger book, and possibly several volumes! To even attempt to tell such a complex story is way beyond the scope of this book. Cheryl Baker said it best when she told Terry and Tiffany DuFoe of *CRAGG Live* in December 2018:

> Honestly, there should be a book. There should be a series on TV, I tell you. The drama that has happened in the Bucks Fizz story, really from day one. There were affairs, there were fights, there was a terrible coach crash when people almost died. There were the glory days of winning the Eurovision and being number one in the charts, and the disastrous days. Scroll forward, and here we are, the fight over the name, who gets the name Bucks Fizz, going to court, and now Jay has had cancer of the tongue. Honestly, if you put all the drama that's happened (to) Bucks Fizz in a book, you'd think 'No, it's too extreme. No one would have a life like that'. But it's true. Our career has been painted with real highs and desperate lows. Too many to talk about.

I wanted the focus of this book to be on the group's music, their singles, albums and videos. The story of Bucks Fizz deserves its own book and can really only be told with insight, balance and integrity by the group members themselves and by those close to them.

All of the Bucks Fizz albums were released at a time when vinyl and cassette were the dominant formats. The related tracks can often be found spread across several CDs, so I have endeavoured to group all of these together for each album. Similarly, Bobby and Cheryl issued solo singles whilst in Bucks Fizz, but solo tracks from Bobby, Cheryl and Shelley also appeared on *The Lost Masters* or on compilations under the Bucks Fizz name. Rather than blur the lines between solo tracks and those by the group, I have given the group's solo material its own section (see Appendix 4).

I have attempted to cover all of the contemporary remixes, unreleased tracks and alternate versions. There isn't space in a book of this size to cover all of the newly created remixes, too, as much as I would like to and as excellent as some of them are, so I have listed them in their own section along with the albums where they can be found (see Appendix 5).

Finally, no one is perfect, and certainly not me! I have discovered new things about Bucks Fizz in the process of writing this book. There have been many times when I have felt unequal to the task. I have also endeavoured to write a kind book. If I have omitted something important in my attempts to do this, then please forgive me.

Would you like to write for Sonicbond Publishing?

At Sonicbond Publishing we are always on the look-out for authors, particularly for our two main series:

On Track. Mixing fact with in depth analysis, the On Track series examines the work of a particular musical artist or group. All genres are considered from easy listening and jazz to 60s soul to 90s pop, via rock and metal.

On Screen. This series looks at the world of film and television. Subjects considered include directors, actors and writers, as well as entire television and film series. As with the On Track series, we balance fact with analysis.

While professional writing experience would, of course, be an advantage the most important qualification is to have real enthusiasm and knowledge of your subject. First-time authors are welcomed, but the ability to write well in English is essential.

Sonicbond Publishing has distribution throughout Europe and North America, and all books are also published in E-book form. Authors will be paid a royalty based on sales of their book.

Further details are available from www.sonicbondpublishing.co.uk. To contact us, complete the contact form there or email info@sonicbondpublishing.co.uk

on track ...

Bucks Fizz

Contents

Introduction

The story of Bucks Fizz begins in late 1980. It starts with a young songwriter named Andy Hill, three former members of the group Rags and two songs: 'Making Your Mind Up' and 'Have You Ever Been In Love'. Rags were a vocal trio comprised of Steve Glen, Nichola Martin and Jill Shirley. In 1977, they entered the Song For Europe with a song called 'Promises, Promises' and released five singles between 1977 and 1980. Although Rags disbanded in 1980, the group members remained in touch as they began branching out in different directions. Steve Glen moved into songwriting and production, recording a solo album and working with other artists; Jill Shirley ventured into management, opening the Razzamatazz agency in London; and Nichola Martin embarked on a professional and personal relationship with Andy Hill and formed the music publishing company Big Note Music Ltd.

In a Radio One interview from 1983, Andy Hill described the two songs he submitted for the Song For Europe, 'Making Your Mind Up' and 'Have You Ever Been In Love', as the third and fourth ones he had ever written. 'Making Your Mind Up' was initially an instrumental backing track in the possession of Nichola Martin that she encouraged Andy Hill to write a song around. Andy Hill enlisted the help of a guitarist he had worked with named John Danter, who was subsequently credited as co-writer of 'Making Your Mind Up'. When the demo of 'Making Your Mind Up' was recorded, it featured vocals by Andy Hill, Nichola Martin and a singer Nichola already knew named Mike Nolan. Mike had previously auditioned for a group that Nichola was in, called Love Together, in 1974, and they had remained in touch since then. From 1977 to 1980, Mike had been a member of the vocal group Brooks, but a chance conversation led to Nichola contacting him to ask for his help in recording the demo of 'Making Your Mind Up', as Mike told Me'shah Bryan on the *Stage And Screen* podcast in 2025:

> She (Nichola Martin) was up at Polydor Records having lunch with someone from the record company, and he was telling her about this group he had let go, a group called Brooks. She said, 'Who's in that band, Brooks? That rings a bell', and he gave my name, the one he remembered. She said, 'I know him. He tried to get into Love Together'. So, she phoned me up and said, 'We're entering some songs for *Song For Europe*, and I wondered if you wanted to come to the studios and help us do the demos for the entries?' I said, 'Yeah, of course I'll do that for you.' We went up to the studio, and it was a Saturday morning. We did it verse by verse, got it down, put all the harmonies in there and finished it. Nichola said, 'That was really good, Mike; if the song gets through, I'll put you in the group.' Anyway, the song was accepted. She said, 'We want you to be in the band. You might as well be in it, Mike; it's another thing to put on your CV. It's *Song For Europe,* and let's face it, 'Making Your Mind Up' will never win it anyway.'

The demo of 'Making Your Mind Up' featuring Mike Nolan, Andy Hill and Nichola Martin had been submitted for the Song For Europe, with Nichola writing the name of the artist as 'Bucks Fizz' on the entry form. At the point 'Making Your Mind Up' was accepted for the 1981 Song For Europe, 'Bucks Fizz' was only a name on a sheet of paper and the group themselves did not exist. Nichola Martin now had to put a group together who could perform 'Making Your Mind Up' at the Song For Europe on 11 March 1981. Mike Nolan had already helped to record the demo of 'Making Your Mind Up', and Nichola had asked him to be a part of the group should the song prove to be successful in progressing to the Song For Europe final. Mike Nolan, therefore, became the first member of Bucks Fizz, and the group was built around him.

Cheryl Baker was the next person to be approached to join Bucks Fizz. Like Mike Nolan, she did not have to audition for the group, and her journey to being a member of Bucks Fizz began with a chance meeting. Cheryl was born Rita Crudgington. She left school at 16 and became a secretary, but her love of music led her to join a local amateur operatic society and sing with a couple of bands (including the wonderfully named Bressingham Spire). Her professional break came in 1975 when she replied to an advertisement and successfully auditioned for the vocal harmony group Mother's Pride (who shortly afterwards would change their name to Co Co). The group had already released two singles on Pye Records, and in the summer of 1975, they had a residency at Blackpool Opera House as part of 'The Freddie Starr Show', a variety show headlined by Freddie Starr which included Mike Burton, Lynn Rogers, Francis Van Dyke, Mothers Pride, The Mistins and The Second Generation Dancers on the bill. Following their change of name to Co Co, the group would appear at the 1976 Song For Europe (finishing in second place) before representing the United Kingdom at the 1978 Eurovision Song Contest with 'Bad Old Days' (finishing 11th). By 1980, times were hard for the group, as Cheryl told Barbara Michaels, 'Work in England had been getting less and less because basically we were a cabaret band and cabaret venues here were closing down and opening up again as discotheques. We got work abroad, we were in a hotel in Finland for six weeks, and we took it because we needed the money.' In June 1980, Cheryl left Co Co and took a job working for Mayfair Sound Studios in London. Speaking to the Lewis Nicholls *Life Stories* podcast in 2024, she said:

> I left Co Co in the summer of 1980. I'd had enough, and I went to work for Mayfair Sound. I typed their letters, as that's what I was trained for; I did their invoices, and I was there to do backing vocals if anyone needed it. One day, in walked Nichola Martin and she said, 'Cheryl, why are you here?' and I said, 'I've left Co Co'. So, she obviously logged this. This would have been probably September, October time, and just before Christmas of 1980, I received a phone call to say that she wanted me to be in this band called Bucks Fizz.

In the meantime, the other song that Andy Hill had submitted for the Song For Europe, 'Have You Ever Been In Love', had also been accepted, with the name of the artist written on the entry form as 'Gem'. For a while, Nichola Martin contemplated putting herself in Bucks Fizz alongside Mike and Cheryl, but on reflection chose to be a member of 'Gem' with Andy Hill. Her decision left two vacancies in the Bucks Fizz lineup needing to be filled, so Nichola turned to her former Rags bandmate Jill Shirley. Jill had opened the Razzamatazz agency in London, representing young singers, dancers, drama school graduates and musical theatre performers. Razzamatazz sent anyone on their books who might be suitable to Nichola to audition. They had to be a similar height to Mike Nolan, be good-looking, blonde or prepared to go blonde, and be able to sing. One of these was 19-year-old Jay Aston, who was on their books as a singer and dancer. She came from a showbiz family as her parents and elder brother were all in the business, and Jay performed her first summer season in Skegness aged just 14. 'I've never really considered anything else but showbiz', she told *Smash Hits* in 1982, 'Either I would teach dancing, keep fit or ballet or something, or be involved in the fashion aspect of it.' Jay had been working in Jersey doing dance classes when the audition for Bucks Fizz came up:

> I did the audition in Nichola Martin's front room, and Mike Nolan was already in the band. They wanted us to fit around him, being quite petite and blonde. I didn't really want the job if I'm completely honest, and I was really happy with what I was lining up in Jersey. I was asked to go back, and I met Andy Hill. We went into a studio just off Oxford Street, and I learned my harmony – I'm usually on the third harmony – I put it down, and they basically offered me the job there and then. (*Vinyl Vibes* podcast, 2024)

The final place in the group was originally offered to Stephen Fischer, who later became one half of the 1982 Song For Europe winners, Bardo. He declined the offer due to a prior contractual commitment to a touring production of *Godspell,* and so an advert was placed in *The Stage,* which resulted in Bobby G (Robert Gubby) joining the group. Bobby had built up his own building firm in the early 1970s, but as the recession hit the trade, he returned to music, playing the cabaret circuit. 1980 saw Bobby playing Pontius Pilate in the West End production of *Jesus Christ Superstar,* which was scheduled to go on tour in the new year. The Bucks Fizz audition came during a convenient gap in his schedule, as he told the *Here She Is* podcast in 2024:

> My Dad phoned up and pushed me to go and do it. It didn't really sound much to be fair. I went up for the audition, which was with Andy Hill, and Mike (Nolan) was there. At the time, there was no money in it, and I just had a gap. I thought, 'It's a couple of months out of my life, I'll go and learn a

> song.' I was quite keen to do some recording in the recording studio, as that's not something I had ever done. When I got (the place in Bucks Fizz), it was, 'I'll do the song, I'll do the performance and (then) I'll go back to my job.'

Mike and Cheryl first met on 7 January 1981 at Nichola Martin's house in Fulham. Four days later, Bucks Fizz met each other for the first time, as Cheryl related on the *Sliding Doors* podcast in 2023, 'We all met on Sunday 11 January. I went along to Nichola's house, and the others were already there. I went into her living room, and she said, 'This is Bobby, this is Jay, you already know Mike: you four are Bucks Fizz.'

Bucks Fizz (1981)

Personnel:
Mike Nolan: lead vocals, backing vocals
Cheryl Baker: lead vocals, backing vocals
Bobby G: lead vocals, backing vocals
Jay Aston: lead vocals, backing vocals
Andy Hill: keyboards, bass, acoustic guitar, backing vocals
Graham Broad: drums
Ian Bairnson: guitar, bass
Mel Collins: lead saxophone
Howey Casey: lead saxophone
Nichola Martin: backing vocals.
Alan Carvell: backing Vocals
Recorded at Mayfair Studios, London, and Morgan Studios, London, between March and July 1981
Mixed at Mayfair Studios, London
Producer: Andy Hill
Engineers: John Hudson, Martin Webster
Photography: Brian Aris
Logo: Rory Kee
Art direction: Andrew Christian
UK release date: July 1981
Charts: UK: 14

The next few months were a whirlwind. Exactly two months after their first meeting, Bucks Fizz had stormed to victory in the Song For Europe. Four weeks later, the group had won the 1981 Eurovision Song Contest and were in demand across the continent. Jill Shirley recalls going to the offices of RCA on the Monday following the group's Eurovision victory and finding RCA's international office covered with telexes from all over Europe, all wanting Bucks Fizz to be on their programmes. They flew out the following Wednesday, going from country to country. In a quote attributed to Cheryl in Simon Garfield's book *Expensive Habits,* she talks about the intensity of those early months:

> When we said 'Yes, we will be a part of Bucks Fizz' and signed the contracts, then that was it. The next day, we had rehearsals, then dance routines, recording the song (because, at that time, it was still just a demo). Then we won *Song For Europe,* which straight away meant television in England and doing promo films for Eurovision and rushing all over the place and making personal appearances. Then Eurovision – bang! We won that, and then you're doing the same as you did in England, and you're doing it all over Europe. You're doing personal appearances in Germany, France, Austria, everywhere. Really, in that first six months, your life isn't your own – you're whisked off, and you eat, drink and sleep Bucks Fizz. Although we were

thrown together like that and had to do all that work just because we were successful, we didn't actually have time to know each other, not until we slowed down, sat back and said, 'Oh, hello, I'm pleased to meet you.'

The group would learn the material for this album while on board coaches, aeroplanes and in hotel rooms, and scheduled recordings around an already hectic schedule. A review of one of the group's later albums talked about Bucks Fizz 'losing their identity' but, for me, the group are still establishing it on this album. 'Making Your Mind Up' existed before the group did, and apart from 'The Right Situation' that closes this album, it is not a style that they ever revisited. Tracks such as 'Piece Of The Action', 'Midnight Reservation' and 'One Of Those Nights' showed the group moving away from their Eurovision winner and developing their own style. Crucially, all the singles and the parent album were UK top 20 hits, which ensured the group had a future. Bucks Fizz are all fine singers, but in Andy Hill, they also had an excellent and still maturing songwriter, producer and musician who could shape a diverse collection of songs with craft and care. Reviewing the album in *Record Mirror,* Daniela Soave bemoaned a lack of emotion in the songs, stating, 'I think Bucks Fizz are a load of gutless wonders who perhaps can sing in tune but don't know the meaning of singing with emotion', although she later conceded, 'Bucks Fizz could be good, too, if only they learned to feel their songs.' Paul Du Noyer's review at *New Musical Express* was pleasantly surprising, 'Either I'm going senile, or these M.O.R. pop albums are getting better. I mean, this one doesn't hurt a bit. At least it's no quick, slick, Eurovision cash-in thrown together.'

Original vinyl copies of *Bucks Fizz* in the UK, Australia, South America and some European countries featured a gatefold sleeve. Interesting variations to look out for are the Japanese pressing with a lyric insert, copies from El Salvador and Ecuador on red vinyl and from Venezuela on orange vinyl. The album was first released on CD in 2004 with contemporary bonus tracks, plus some material recorded in 1985 and 1988, and selected tracks from the group's Spanish language album *El Mundo De Ilusion*. The 2015 'Definitive Edition' includes bonus tracks from 1981, demos from *Lost Masters 2* and some newly created remixes, whilst disc two features the Spanish language album in full.

From complete strangers at the start of January to Eurovision victory, international success, three hit singles and a top 20 album by mid-September. *Bucks Fizz* encapsulates the group's successful first phase, but their biggest-selling UK single and highest-charting album were just around the corner.

'Piece Of The Action' (Andy Hill)

Released as a single in May 1981. Chart place: UK: 12.

In the years immediately preceding Bucks Fizz winning the Eurovision Song Contest, follow-up singles to UK Eurovision entries had not fared well. Prima

Donna finished third in 1980, but their second single, 'Just Got To Be You', failed to chart, and the group went their separate ways. 'Mary Ann' gave Black Lace their first taste of UK chart success in 1979, but their follow-up, 'So Long Suzi Baby', was not a hit, and their reinvention as a duo and purveyors of party tunes was still four years away. Co Co, who represented the UK in 1978, released two further singles that year, 'I Can't Talk Love On The Telephone Line' and 'Way Out', without success. Even Brotherhood Of Man, who had romped to victory in 1976 and been number one for six weeks with 'Save Your Kisses For Me', had initially faltered when their soundalike follow-up 'My Sweet Rosalie' only reached number 30 and had to endure a couple of non-charting singles before 'Oh Boy (The Mood I'm In)' restored them to the top ten. 'Piece Of The Action', then, is a pop music masterclass: a genuinely great pop song that appealed to the same fans who had bought 'Making Your Mind Up' whilst simultaneously being a quite different kind of song that moved the group's sound and image forward. In *The Bucks Fizz Story* DVD, former RCA Executive Bill Kimber observed:

> One of the things that happens with Eurovision winners is that they have one single as a result of the contest, and then they quickly throw out another record that isn't good enough, and everybody forgets them. What we did deliberately (with Bucks Fizz) was work really hard at making sure that the second single was a song that was good value radio-wise, commercially, and was well-produced.

In many ways, 'Piece Of The Action' became the making of Bucks Fizz. The success of 'Making Your Mind Up' had given the group a platform, but the group had been created to perform the song. 'Piece Of The Action' is where the group start to find their own identity and it displays many of the strengths of those early Bucks Fizz records: Andy Hill's gift for melody and his skill as a producer; a small group of world-class musicians who are not only able to execute Andy Hill's ideas but enhance and embellish them with their own ability; four strong vocalists in Bucks Fizz themselves, each with different styles and strengths, all of whom can sing lead and can harmonise with each other in differing combinations and, on this track, the backing vocals of Andy Hill, Alan Carvell and Nichola Martin provide a contrast to the group's vocals in the chorus. There is a joyfulness about 'Piece Of The Action', and it is an excellent pop song that still stands up today. It entered the UK charts at number 57 in June 1981, with 'Making Your Mind Up' still in the top 40 and rose to number 12 during a nine-week run. It climbed 32 places to number 25 during its second week, leading to the group appearing on *Top Of The Pops* to perform this song on 11 June 1981 (Episode 896). The group also made their first of many appearances on the children's pop music show *Razzmatazz* on 14 July 1981 (Episode 7), as well as shows in Europe and Australasia, where the song became a top 40 hit. The promotional video featured some black and white sections with a retro 1960s theme, and the group performing the routine to the song in a nightclub setting whilst wearing khaki outfits, a decision taken by Nichola Martin and a look that carried over to the photoshoot for the *Bucks Fizz* album cover.

The single was issued in a picture sleeve with another track from the forthcoming album, 'Took It To The Limit', as the B-side. Following the group's international success, it was issued in multiple territories, so, for collectors, there are lots of international variations to look out for, chief among these are a red vinyl pressing from El Salvador which features 'Shine On' as the B-side, and two different one sided Australian promos entitled 'Your Piece Of The Action' (RCA PROMO 54) containing excerpts of four tracks from the album, and 'Peter's Ice Cream, The 'Piece Of The Action' Promotion' (RCA PROMO 55), which highlights details of their promotional campaign, followed by the track itself.

A surprising number of Bucks Fizz songs have been covered by other artists over the years, and 'Piece Of The Action' became one of them when the Bay City Rollers released it as a Japanese-only single in 1983.

'Midnight Reservation' (Andy Hill/Pete Sinfield)

Those who casually dismiss Bucks Fizz might be surprised to see the name Pete Sinfield featuring regularly in the group's songwriting credits. Peter Sinfield (1943-2024) was a founder member of King Crimson and wrote the lyrics for their early albums, including their seminal debut, *In The Court Of The Crimson King*. He went on to produce the debut album for Roxy Music and their dazzling hit single 'Virginia Plain' and released a solo album entitled *Still* in 1973 before linking up with former King Crimson bandmate Greg Lake and beginning a fruitful songwriting partnership with Emerson, Lake & Palmer. Peter also wrote the lyrics for two songs that, in my view, are among the finest Christmas songs ever made: Greg Lake's 'I Believe In Father Christmas' and Chris Squire and Alan White's 'Run With The Fox'.

His songwriting collaboration with Andy Hill extends before and beyond Bucks Fizz and begins with his other 1981 Song For Europe entry: 'Have You Ever Been In Love'. Andy Hill wrote the song with John Danter, but when he submitted it to his publishers, they requested a revision of the lyrics and suggested he work with Pete Sinfield. 'Have You Ever Been In Love' subsequently became a hit for Leo Sayer (UK: 10) and went on to win an Ivor Novello award in 1983. Andy Hill and Pete Sinfield repeated this achievement in 1995 with their song 'Think Twice', which was a massive international hit and a UK number one for Celine Dion.

This is their first joint songwriting credit on a Bucks Fizz record, and it is a well-crafted melodic pop song that sits in perfectly behind 'Piece Of The Action'. The lyrics deal lightly with miscommunication in a somewhat tempestuous relationship. In keeping with the train imagery of the song, the steady, rhythmic feel of the verses is accentuated by the clever way the lyrics are sung, with brief pauses within lines and even within individual words (listen to the way Mike and Bobby sing the lines 'I've Got a feeling I've been dreaming, I've been here before/She believes that I've been knocking on another door'). Towards the end of the song, there is a pleasing overlapping of three different vocal lines; first the backing vocals, then Cheryl and Jay, then Mike and Bobby, with Ian Bairnson's guitar filling in the spaces as the song fades.

'It's Got To Be Love' (Andy Hill/A. Nicholas)
With no solo vocals for them on *Bucks Fizz,* Mike and Cheryl perform a duet on this beautiful ballad. It is unashamedly romantic and middle of the road, but, as Richard Carpenter once rightly observed, just because a song is middle of the road does not necessarily mean that it is bland, and this song isn't. Mike and Cheryl's voices complement each other as they share the two verses before the sumptuous, soft harmonies of the chorus, interspersed by a gentle classical guitar solo two-thirds of the way through. The group later recorded a Spanish language version of the track, 'Yo Se Que Es Amor', which was paired with a Spanish version of 'Shine On', entitled 'Brillar', and released as a single in Spain, Mexico, Argentina, The Philippines, Chile, El Salvador and Peru. The Spanish and Mexican versions each had different picture sleeves, whilst the copies from El Salvador were again pressed on red vinyl.

At Mike Nolan's final gig with The Fizz in November 2024, Mike and Cheryl performed this song. The close friendship between the two of them, and the love that Fizz fans have always had for both of them, goes right back to the start of the group. It was a sweet and touching moment.

'Took It To The Limit' (Andy Hill/Nichola Martin)
A synthesised Giorgio Moroder esque rhythm runs through this song, one of two flirtations with disco on the album, and it stands in contrast to the two ballads on either side of it. It is a track that Bucks Fizz fans were already familiar with as it appeared on the B-side of 'Piece Of The Action' ahead of the album's release. There is an effective layering of the vocals throughout the song, with different voices coming to prominence. The verses are softer, with first the backing vocals from Andy Hill, Alan Carvell and Nichola Martin clearly audible, before Cheryl's light, delicate harmonies emerge, building up to the chorus. The chorus vocals are more forceful, with first Mike and Bobby and then Jay being the focal point. The addition of a brass section is unobtrusive but adds colour to the track and punctuates the gaps between the vocals. There is even time for a guitar solo from the ever-wonderful Ian Bairnson and some breathy, whispered vocals during the breakdown. Although other tracks have superseded it with time, this was one of my initial favourites on the album. I always thought that 'Took It To The Limit' deserved to have an extended version, and as a young teenager, I even crassly tried to create one by editing sections of the song together on cassette. Fortunately, it

was done properly 42 years later, when an extended remix was created and included on *The Land Of Make Believe – The Definitive Collection*.

'One Of Those Nights' (Steve Glen/Mike Burns/Dave Most)
Released as a single in August 1981. Chart place: UK: 20.
Prior to putting Bucks Fizz together, Nichola Martin had her own experience of the Song For Europe as part of the vocal trio Rags, whose line-up consisted of Nichola Martin, Steve Glen and future Bucks Fizz manager Jill Shirley. Their entry in the 1977 Song For Europe, 'Promises Promises', came fourth (the eventual winners of the competition were Lynsey De Paul and Mike Moran with 'Rock Bottom') and, despite an appearance on *Top Of The Pops,* 'Promises Promises' was not a hit.

Rags went on to win the World Song Festival with another song entitled 'Can't Hide My Love', but after three further singles ('How Can I Exist', 'Honey Honey' and 'Night Music'), the group were no more. March 1980 saw Nichola Martin in the Song For Europe as a member of Duke and The Aces (whose lineup also included future *Strictly Come Dancing* judge Bruno Tonioli), and Steve Glen had established a songwriting partnership with Mike Burns and David Most. Together, they penned nine of the ten tracks on Steve's 1980 solo album *Look Left, Look Right,* and worked on a number of side projects (of particular interest to Fizz fans is the second single by The Toys, 'Easy Does It'. It was co-written with Andy Hill and features Nichola Martin in the video. Quite why it was not a hit in 1980 beats me). They also wrote top 40 hits for Kandidate ('I Don't Wanna Lose You' and 'Girls Girls Girls') and scored a monster hit with Hot Chocolate's 'No Doubt About It'. Their joint songwriting contribution to this album, 'One Of Those Nights', was the third single lifted from the album and was a stylistic departure for Bucks Fizz. It was their first single to feature a single member of the group, in this instance Bobby, as a lead vocalist, and it also represented a change of pace after two ebullient, upbeat singles.

The song is a moody mid-paced ballad about a man yearning for a former lover. He is unable to sleep, haunted by her memory and trying to comprehend why the relationship broke up. For me, it is one of the highlights of the group's debut album: classy, dramatic and beautifully structured. The guitars and keyboards in the introduction fall away to create a suitably sparse opening verse consisting of subdued keyboards, drums, bass and solo vocal, gradually building up to the group harmonies in the chorus before receding again. Particularly effective are the wordless vocal harmonies that gently, yet repeatedly, precede the lines 'I'm living in the shadows/I've got nowhere to go', creating an impression of memories returning.

There was no promotional video for this single, although the group appeared on *Top Of The Pops* to perform this track once, initially broadcast on 3 September 1981 (Episode 908) and repeated on Thursday 17 September 1981. The picture sleeve of the 7" single uses the same image of the group found on their album cover and was backed by a non-album track, 'Always

Thinking Of You'. The song gave the group their third consecutive hit, climbing to number 20 in the UK.

It is also worth highlighting that, following the relative commercial disappointment of their sophomore album, *The Paris Collection,* Dollar recorded a demo version of 'One Of Those Nights' prior to Bucks Fizz recording it. Their version is included in the *Ultimate Dollar* box set, with Thereza Bazar remarking in the sleeve notes, 'What a terrific song! I wish we had finished the track and made it our sound.' I am sure 'One Of Those Nights' would have been a hit for Dollar, but in truth, the song was a much better fit for Bucks Fizz and for Bobby G's vocal style. In any case, Dollar would soon embark on their own run of magnificent pop singles, produced and co-written by Trevor Horn.

'Making Your Mind Up' (Andy Hill/John Danter)
Released as a single in March 1981. Chart place: UK: 1.

> 'If you believe that a love can hit the top you gotta play around'? What does that mean? Honestly, it's nonsense … But, you know, thank goodness for it! Where would I be without 'Making Your Mind Up'?'
> Cheryl Baker (*Beyond The Title* podcast, 2023)

The first time the general public would have seen Bucks Fizz or heard 'Making Your Mind Up' was on *A* Song For Europe in 1981, held at the BBC Television Theatre in Shepherd's Bush on Wednesday 11 March 1981. On the night, Bucks Fizz swept to victory, receiving maximum points from five of the seven juries, dropping only eight points, and finishing 27 points clear of runners-up Liquid Gold with their song, 'Don't Panic'. Liquid Gold were the best-known name in the competition, with four hit singles behind them. Tom Marshall, who had previously been a member of M Squad with Steve Stroud in the 1979 Song For Europe and would later become a member of Bucks Fizz's touring band, was recruited by Liquid Gold for their performance in the contest. In his book, *Catch A Falling Star,* he recalls:

> We watched all of the acts one by one throughout the afternoon live rehearsals. As each act performed, we were not that impressed and thought that we had a good chance to win. When it was our turn, 'Don't Panic' was really well received by the TV engineers. We sat down again to watch the next act. They were called Bucks Fizz, and their song was 'Making Your Mind Up'. This did sound good, but when the boys ripped the girls' skirts off before the last chorus, our jaws dropped, we all sighed, looked at each other and thought, 'Oops … that's the end of 'Don't Panic' and Liquid Gold.'

Steve Stroud was part of the group Beyond, who finished third with their song 'Wish'. In *The Bucks Fizz Story* DVD, he expresses a similar sentiment, 'We were very confident in the song because we thought it was one of the best ballads we'd heard. When we heard the Fizz song, we weren't that impressed. Then, on the dress rehearsal day, Fizz did their fantastic rip the skirts off and … quite frankly, I think we all held our hands up and said, 'That's it'.

The 'skirt rip' has passed into Eurovision folklore, and it is still remembered (and imitated) over four decades later. It became the showstopping moment, the staging that made the performance stand out from all the others, though whose idea it was is disputed. In *The Bucks Fizz Story* DVD, Nichola Martin laid claim to the idea, and Bobby G likewise recalls it originating with her. However, the most common consensus attributes it to choreographer Chrissy Wickham, stemming from a discussion about clothes, and whether Cheryl and Jay should wear long skirts (as Cheryl preferred) or short skirts (as Jay suggested), as Cheryl told the Lewis Nicholls *Life Stories* podcast in 2024:

> Everyone was there, the record label, the production company, the writers, the choreographer and us, the manager. We're all giving a different opinion, and I just went 'Oh, for goodness' sake, let's just have both' … And Chrissy Wickham, the choreographer, went 'That's it! On the line 'If you wanna see some more', we take the top skirt off, and the mini skirt is underneath.' It won us the *Eurovision Song Contest.*

As for the song itself, it began life as a 16-track backing track of an unused song that Steve Glen had been working on. Nichola Martin told the *Here She Is* podcast in 2023, 'I had this backing track … it was actually done for a German band that Steve was producing, and he decided not to do this song. So, I said (to Andy Hill), why don't you write a song for Eurovision around it, and I will submit it through me as a publisher?' According to Gordon Roxburgh's excellent book, *Songs For Europe Volume Three: The Eighties,* Andy Hill collaborated with guitarist John Danter, who was not signed to a publisher but who was subsequently credited as co-writer of 'Making Your Mind Up'. In 2012, a track published by Steve Glen's Blue Melon Records and billed as 'Making Your Mind Up (Original Rhythm Backing Track)' appeared on streaming services. It is worth a listen, as it would appear that this backing track, or something very much like it, was the foundation for this piece of Eurovision history.

'Making Your Mind Up' is a light but lively rock 'n' roll number with a memorable chorus (and routine), but it is fair to say that it provoked a mixed reaction from the UK press at the time. Hilary Bonner, writing in *The Sun,* said, 'The bookies' favourite but not mine. Britain has a good record in the contest, and this well-presented song is sure to be in the running tonight. But, to me, it sounds like a record you heard years ago and didn't bother to buy.' David Hepworth, writing in *Smash Hits,* commented, 'This is actually our entry for the Eurovision Alliteration Contest, a record so deeply moronic that they must already be throwing in the towel from Monaco to Munchen.'

Charles Catchpole remarked that the record sounded dated; however, rock 'n' roll revivals were doing well on the UK charts at that time, with Bucks Fizz surging past Coast To Coast's '(Do) The Hucklebuck' as it climbed the charts and deposing Shakin' Stevens on their way to the number one spot.

The 1981 Eurovision Song Contest was held at the Simmonscourt Pavilion in Dublin on 4 April 1981. The voting was close and incredibly tense. Bucks Fizz did not score spectacularly – they only received maximum votes from Israel and the Netherlands – but they scored consistently and were the only country to pick up votes from every jury. With two countries left to vote, three countries were tied in first place with 120 points: Germany, Switzerland, and the United Kingdom. Switzerland were the penultimate country to vote and so could not award votes to themselves. They proceeded to award eight votes for the United Kingdom but nothing for Germany, putting Bucks Fizz eight points clear with one vote left. It all came down to Sweden, who awarded one point to Switzerland and a maximum 12 points to Germany, but they also allocated eight points to the UK, ensuring that Bucks Fizz won the Eurovision Song Contest on the final vote by four points.

Following their Eurovision success, the song became a massive international hit, going to number one not only in the UK but also in Austria, Belgium, Denmark, Ireland, Israel, the Netherlands and Spain. The song also became a top ten hit in Australia, Finland, Germany, New Zealand, Norway, South Africa, Sweden and Switzerland. Surprisingly, the UK 7" did not have a picture sleeve (the only Bucks Fizz single not to do so), but there is a wealth of unique international picture sleeves to track down from Belgium, Brazil, Finland, Germany, Italy, Japan, the Netherlands, Portugal, Spain and former Yugoslavia.

The group shot a video for the Eurovision Song Contest previews at Harrods department store in Kensington, which was broadcast on the BBC on 29 March 1981. Bucks Fizz made their *Top Of The Pops* debut on 19 March 1981 (Episode 884) and made a second appearance following their Eurovision victory on 9 April 1981 (Episode 887). These two clips were repeated every week from 19 March to 23 April inclusive, with the group's preview video being shown for their third week at number one on 30 April 1981 (Episode 890). The group also appeared on *Cheggers Plays Pop* on 6 April, *The Val Doonican Show* on 11 April and numerous shows worldwide over the coming months, including *Top Pop, Countdown, Aplauso, Chansons A La Carte* and *WWF Club.* Later that year, the group performed a live version of the song at a charity event in Mysen near Oslo called the *Momarkedet,* organised annually by the Red Cross. The 1981 event featured Eurovision Song Contest winners from 1956 to 1981 and was first broadcast on TV in the UK on 25 September 1981, with Terry Wogan introducing the highlights, and later on BBC Radio 2 on Boxing Day 1981.

In a 1984 interview with *Look In,* Jay commented, 'I must admit I'm not really keen on 'Making Your Mind Up'. I mean, I love it for what it did for us;

it made us. So, it's a bit of a love-hate relationship now with all of us, really.' 'Making Your Mind Up' is a bright, colourful, fun, lightweight rock 'n' roll number. The group, the song and the routine appealed to an international audience, and it became an iconic moment in Eurovision history. Personally, I love the song for winning Eurovision for the United Kingdom, for being my introduction to Bucks Fizz, for the memories it elicits and the nostalgia. I love all of the references in pop culture, from *Miranda* right up to Remember Monday's little tribute to it in their fabulous performance at the 2025 Eurovision Song Contest, but the song is far from being one of my favourite Bucks Fizz tracks. However, it became the launch pad for everything that followed, so thank heavens for it. Where would Bucks Fizz, their fans or Eurovision be without it?

'Lady Of The Night' (Nichola Martin)

The only Bucks Fizz song that is credited solely to Nichola Martin. The verses are sung from two different lyrical perspectives. The male vocals are subjective, expressing that the 'midnight love affair' is based on an irresistible yet emotionally damaging attraction. The female vocals that follow offer a dispassionate, objective view of the woman who is portrayed as evasive and deceitful and has 'nothing in her soul'. The lyrics are wrapped up in a catchy, upbeat pop song with some lovely harmonies, especially in the verses. It also benefits from a short keyboard and saxophone break after the second chorus.

'Lady Of The Night' would go on to have another lease of life a year later when it was covered by Bardo and appeared on the B-side of their 1982 Eurovision entry 'One Step Further'. Bardo's version has a slightly different arrangement, with solo voices in the verses and Stephen Fischer and Sally Ann Triplett trading alternate lines, which necessitates a minor lyric change. The Bardo version is also shorter than the Bucks Fizz original, as it dispenses with the instrumental break.

'Getting Kinda Lonely' (Mike Burns/Robert Parr)

This song had quite an eventful life. It was written by musician, songwriter and producer Bob Parr, who would later work as an engineer on the *Are You Ready* album, and Mike Burns, who, along with Steve Glen and Dave Most, had written 'One Of Those Nights' for this album. 'Getting Kinda Lonely' was actually a cover version. It was first released as a single in 1980 by Swiss musician and songwriter Corry Knobel (billed simply as 'Corry'), a version which Steve Glen co-produced. In 1982, Bucks Fizz recorded a Spanish-language version of the track, 'Hoy Siento Soledades', which was released as a single in Argentina. This, in turn, resulted in a fine cover version in 1983, 'Me Estoy Sintiendo Sola' by Venezuelan 'Queen of Rock' Melissa (Melissa Mariana Griffiths Parra Del Riego), which became a hit in Latin America when it featured as the theme to the telenovelas *Virginia* and *Julia*. It is all quite an exotic journey for a Bucks Fizz album track.

The song is the only solo lead vocal for Jay Aston on this album. In an interview with *Record Mirror* in 1982, she remarked that she had struggled to make an emotional connection with the song, 'I must admit when Andy (Hill) first played 'Getting Kinda Lonely' to me, I thought, 'Oh no, oh dear, I can't feel it." Despite this, Jay gives this old school ballad her all, expressing vulnerability in the gentle beginnings of each verse before shifting gear into a powerful vocal. There are some excellent harmonies during the chorus, and a beautiful instrumental section at the end that borrows elements of 10cc's 'I'm Not In Love'. It fades out far too early, although an unedited version was included on *Lost Masters 2* many years later. TV footage of the group performing this song (and 'The Land Of Make Believe') on the Bravo oil production platform off the Scottish coast for Russell Harty's BBC2 show was first broadcast on 25 February 1982 and can be found online.

'Shine On' (Andy Hill/Nichola Martin)
A joyous, uplifting piece of disco-infused pop that extolls the virtues of positivity. The twinkling keyboards and electric guitars glide over a light dance groove, with Bobby and Cheryl's voices at the forefront in the verses as the backing vocals in the chorus urge the listener to 'push those cloudy days away'. This is one of my favourite tracks on the album, but I would also highlight two cover versions of this song. One was in 1982 by Orient Express, which pushed the song even further in a dance-soul direction. The other was a single release in 1981 by Celena Duncan, also produced by Andy Hill, which is a much funkier and heavily synthesised affair. I draw attention to these because there is some confusion over the lyrics to 'Shine On', especially the last line of the first verse. A quick Google search brings up some best guesses (e.g. 'Accusing me of acting like her father') and even the lyric sheet on the Japanese pressing of the album leaves this line blank. The lyrics are pronounced more distinctly on the two cover versions and on Celena Duncan's Andy Hill-produced version are 'You seem bent on acting like a martyr'. Orient Express changed the word 'bent' to 'set', but, on balance, I am calling the lyrics on Celena's version definitive.

'The Right Situation' (Andy Hill/Pete Sinfield/Buick)
If 'Making Your Mind Up' had a twin, then it would be 'The Right Situation'. The structure of the song in its initial stages is very similar to the group's Eurovision winner. It begins with the main hookline sung by the group, which is then repeated with different lyrics sung by Bobby and Mike. A second melody is then introduced, sung by the whole group, before returning to the first melody, again with different lyrics, followed by an instrumental break. It is a bouncy little track that ends the album on a positive note and appeals to fans who loved 'Making Your Mind Up' and came looking for more of the same. It sounds like the group had fun recording it, and it makes me smile for that reason. Having said that, it is not the type of music I listen to,

either then or now, so I am pleased that it's a style the group swiftly moved away from.

Related Tracks

Five tracks were added to the 2015 *Bucks Fizz: The Definitive Edition* CD.

'Don't Stop' (Andy Hill/Nichola Martin)

Originally the B-side to 'Making Your Mind Up', 'Don't Stop' is a lively, innocuous rock 'n' roll number and a suitable companion piece to its Eurovision-winning other half. Worth seeking out is a rare TV performance of the song from 1981 on the Spanish TV Show *Aplauso*.

'Always Thinking Of You' (Andy Hill/Nichola Martin)

A gentle song with some lovely soft harmonies in the verses that originally appeared on the B-side of 'One Of Those Nights', although Andy Hill's arrangement requires Cheryl to hit some incredibly high notes in her lead vocal.

There is another version of this song recorded by Bardo in 1982 that was the B-side to their excellent single, 'Talking Out Of Line'. Their rendition was pitched at a lower key, sung by Sally Ann Triplett and was faster, with a steady beat running through it. However, whilst researching this book, it appears that there may be another earlier version. I had always believed that the first appearance on vinyl of 'Have You Ever Been In Love' was under the name Paris with 'One Touch (Don't Mean Devotion)' on the B-side (Hansa 7), but it appears that there was also a release under the group's original name, Gem, with 'Always Thinking Of You' credited as the B-side (Hansa 3). It would be fascinating to hear this (presumably original) version by Gem to compare it to the other two.

'One Of Those Nights (Demo)' (Steve Glen/Mike Burns/Dave Most)

An early version of the group's third hit, featuring drums, bass, rhythm guitar and piano throughout. The electronic keyboards, subtle shifts in instrumentation and the group's evocative harmonies are yet to come. The keyboard intro is missing, and this version is shorter, with the song's key change coming in the second chorus and omitting the 'I'm living in the shadows/I've got nowhere to go' section that follows it on the album version. This demo also features a dead ending, as opposed to the finished version, which fades out.

'Piece Of The Action (Demo)' (Andy Hill)

A rudimentary version of the track with the verses sung entirely by Mike and the rhythm guitar much higher in the mix. The little touches that made the finished track more dynamic are not quite there yet: the keyboard intro and 'clap' at the start of the song are absent, likewise the guitar and bass part that bring the song to a brief stop before each verse, and the answering backing vocals in the chorus. It is a fascinating snapshot of an excellent pop song in the making.

'The Right Situation (Early Mix)' (Andy Hill/Pete Sinfield/Buick)
A stripped-down version of the album closer, minus the brass parts and with fewer guitars and backing vocals. The 'party' vocals that pervade the track are also less prevalent at the start and quieter in the mix throughout. It was unlikely to be released in this form as it clearly needed more adding to it, but personally, I prefer this mix to the album version.

An additional track appeared on *The Lost Masters 2 – The Final Cut*:

'Getting Kinda Lonely (Unedited Version)' (Mike Burns/Robert Parr)
Exactly the same as the album version, but extending the instrumental section at the end for a further 53 seconds. The drums fade back in, quietly keeping a beat, before the recurring 'strings' melody line brings the song to a dead end.

A further track appeared on *Remixes and Rarities*:

'Making Your Mind Up (Original Multi Track Edit)' (Andy Hill/John Danter)
A shorter rendering of the group's Eurovision winner that edits out the second 'And now you've really gotta speed it up' chorus that occurs at the 2.10 mark on the released version.

Are You Ready (1982)

Personnel:
Mike Nolan: lead vocals, backing vocals
Cheryl Baker: lead vocals, backing vocals
Bobby G: lead vocals, backing vocals
Jay Aston: lead vocals, backing vocals
Andy Hill: keyboards, bass, guitar
Graham Broad: drums and percussion
Ian Bairnson: electric guitar
Pete Willsher: steel guitar
Nick Ingman: string arrangements
Bruce Baxter: brass arrangements
Recorded at Mayfair Studios, London, between 1981 and 1982
Mixed at Mayfair Studios, London, Marcus Studios, London
Producer: Andy Hill
Engineers: John Hudson, Brad Davis, Brian Tench, Bobby Parr
Photography: John Shaw
Sleeve design and art direction: Andrew Christian
UK release date: April 1982
Charts: UK: 10

Following the release of their first album, there was no easing of the pace for Bucks Fizz, with vocal rehearsals at the Prince of Wales Theatre, dance rehearsals, interviews, album signings, photo shoots and TV and radio appearances. The final third of 1981 saw Bucks Fizz promoting a new single and recording a new album whilst travelling the world and touring the UK in support of the previous one.

At the start of November 1981, the group performed at the Yamaha Song Festival in Tokyo, where a new song, 'Another Night', was awarded a grand prize for best song and was subsequently released as a single in Japan. Bucks Fizz travelled to the Philippines and Australia, performing 'Making Your Mind Up' (which had been a top ten hit there) and 'Piece Of The Action' on *Countdown* on 15 November 1981, which thankfully can still be viewed online. The group's first UK tour began at Southport New Theatre on 5 December 1981 and progressed through an especially harsh winter, ending at Brighton Dome on 18 December 1981. Support on the tour came from fellow RCA artist Kate Robbins and Beyond, who had scored a number two hit in the UK earlier that year with 'More Than In Love'. Her backing group, Beyond, had competed in the 1981 Song For Europe alongside Bucks Fizz, and by the time the group hit the road in support of *Are You Ready* the following summer, three members of Beyond (Adrian Sheppard, Steve Stroud and Alan Coates) would be part of the Bucks Fizz touring band.

On the eve of the tour, the group released their fourth single, 'The Land Of Make Believe'. It became the group's biggest-selling single in the UK and gave

Bucks Fizz their second number one, with Jay later telling *Look In*: 'It was our first real number one. Eurovision made 'Making Your Mind Up' number one, really. To reach number one through being just us was something.' Bucks Fizz promoted the song with television appearances throughout December, even cancelling their post-tour Christmas breaks to record an appearance for the Christmas Eve edition of *Top Of The Pops*. Promotion for the single in the UK and Europe continued into January as the group worked on two studio projects: their new record and a Spanish-language album containing tracks from *Bucks Fizz* and their as-yet-untitled new album. In March 1982, 'My Camera Never Lies' was released as the second single; a beautifully crafted modern pop record, far removed from their Eurovision winner of only a year before, that gave Bucks Fizz their third UK number one single. *Are You Ready* was released the following month and became the group's highest charting UK album, reaching number ten. The album received some of the best reviews of the group's career. A glowing 10 out of 10 review from Bev Hellier in *Smash Hits* said:

> Take two good-looking boys, two attractive girls and a selection of songs that Fizz with more pop than a lorry load of 7Up, and this is the result. Although earlier hits like 'The Land Of Make Believe' and 'My Camera Never Lies' are included, these are overshadowed by new material which demonstrates surprising versatility. The title track and '20th Century Hero' are obvious future hits, although one of the ballads, 'Now Those Days Are Gone', could easily combine a new credibility with chart success. Almost the perfect pop album.

In *Record Mirror*, Daniela Soave revised her opinion of the group, opening her four-star review with the words 'Bursting with bounce, Bucks Fizz have got it right. Ten carefully crafted pop songs, full of catchy choruses and middle eights, with a generous dash of emotion – conspicuous by its absence on their debut LP.' Several tracks on *Are You Ready* feature brass and string arrangements, but beyond that, and with the sole exception of 'Love Dies Hard', just three musicians created the album: Andy Hill, Graham Broad and Ian Bairnson. The writing was a similarly tight-knit affair, which gave the album a focus and an identity that its predecessor sometimes lacked. It benefited from a tremendous set of songs that progressed the group's sound, and, perhaps having a greater appreciation of the group's vocal capabilities, Andy Hill pushed them individually and collectively. Jay, Bobby and Mike all have standout solo moments, but in many ways, it is Cheryl Baker's voice that is the sound of this album. Listen to her harmonies on tracks like 'Are You Ready', 'Breaking And Entering', 'My Camera Never Lies', or her gorgeous soft vocals on 'Easy Love' or 'Love Dies Hard', and it is her harmonies that pervade this record and bind it all together.

'One Step Further' was another track that could have ended up on this album, and tapes from Mayfair Studios dated 20 November 1981 contain a 'rough mix with vocals' logged under the name Bucks Fizz. Composer Simon Jefferis had approached the group about the song when they were in an adjacent studio in Clacton, and they gave him the telephone number for Andy Hill. He liked the song and put down a basic version at Mayfair Studios with Simon Jefferis and Graham Broad. Andy Hill wanted to record the track with Bucks Fizz, but Nichola Martin decided to enter it for the 1982 Song For Europe, and the song became a UK hit for Bardo, reaching number two. I think that Bucks Fizz could have done a fine version of the song (Mike on lead vocals, possibly?), and Bobby G provided backing vocals on the Bardo single at the request of Andy Hill, but in fairness, Bucks Fizz had more than enough strong material of their own.

In the UK and Ireland, 'Now Those Days Are Gone' was lifted as the third single from the album and it became a top ten hit in both countries, 'Easy Love' was remixed and released as a single in Denmark and became a top 20 hit there, whilst in parts of Europe and Australasia, 'Are You Ready' was the third single. The group were in Australia for promotion and performed the track and 'My Camera Never Lies' on *Countdown* before commencing a huge UK tour that summer, starting in Bristol on 17 July and ending in St Austell on 30 August.

It was a pleasant and unexpected surprise when *Are You Ready* was released on CD for the first time, 18 years later. The 2000 version omitted 'Takin' Me Higher' and the 12" of 'My Camera Never Lies' but seized the chance to include two previously unreleased tracks from 1983 and 1984, perhaps uncertain that the opportunity for another Bucks Fizz CD would occur again. The 2004 reissue included all three B-sides and the extended mix, plus two tracks from the *You And Your Heart So Blue* and *Talking In Your Sleep* EPs. The 2015 'Definitive Edition' added the alternate version of 'Another Night' and the remix of 'Easy Love' from *Lost Masters 2,* the live version of 'Another Night' from the 1981 Yamaha Song Contest, a dead-end version of 'My Camera Never Lies' and a lot of remixes created between 1991 and 2014.

Q Magazine might have dismissed the 2000 reissue as 'harmless fluff', but, for me, *Are You Ready* is a magnificent pop album that has stood the test of time and one that I still enjoy. If you have heard and liked a Bucks Fizz singles compilation and are not sure where to go next, I would recommend that you start here.

'My Camera Never Lies' (Andy Hill/Nichola Martin)

Released as a single in March 1982. Chart place: UK: 1

Released on 19 March 1982, 'My Camera Never Lies' is a sleek, brilliant, modern pop song with an inventive vocal arrangement that deservedly returned Bucks Fizz to the top of the charts. There is a lot poured into this song: the group's harmonies, Andy Hill's surging bassline, the constant shifts in tempo, Graham Broad's off-the-wall drumming, the complex overlapping vocal lines and a hook that relies not just on the melody but on the unique way the vocals are delivered by the group.

The 7" single was backed by a new track, 'What Am I Gonna Do', and for the first time in the UK, there was also a Bucks Fizz 12" single featuring an extended version of the A-side. Some UK copies of the 7" single came with a poster sleeve, and some of these posters (bearing the 7" catalogue number) were included with selected 12" pressings, too. Most European sleeves were variations on the UK sleeve, except for Spain and France, who used the image from the cover of *Are You Ready*. France also placed 'The Land Of Make Believe' on the B-side, in preference to 'What Am I Gonna Do'.

The group performed the song on *Razzmatazz* on 15 March 1982 (this performance featured a different, still unreleased mix of the song) and on *Starburst* on 17 March 1982 (which was a rerecorded TV mix). Bucks Fizz returned as the interval act for the 1982 Song For Europe and performed the single to a backing track on 23 March 1982, which was inserted into the live show the following day. Later, the group appeared alongside the contest's winners, Bardo, on *Cheggers Plays Pop* on 5 April 1982 (Episode 39) and twice on *Top Of The Pops,* first on 25 March 1982 (Episode 938) when the song was a new entry at number 33, and again on 15 April 1982 (Episode 941) when the single was at number one. On 8 April 1982, the programme aired the promotional video, which featured the group performing the song, intercut with recreations of scenes from classic movies, including *Gone With The Wind, The Seven Year Itch, Cleopatra, The Wizard Of Oz* and *The Wild One*.

Alan Jones, writing in *Record Mirror,* asserted that Bucks Fizz had improved beyond recognition and 'Their recent output has comprised some of the most superbly crafted songs to grace the chart this decade.' Others disagreed, however, with Dave Rimmer in *Smash Hits* stating, 'Don't this lot have any new ideas? Same old oompah-oompah rhythm, clean wholesome vocals and utterly pathetic lyrics … sorry Fizz fans, this is horrible.' I was of the former opinion. I thought that the group were progressing in leaps and bounds and that this was their best single to date. Four decades on, and this is still one of the group's best tracks and a great way to start a superb album.

'Easy Love' (Andy Hill/Nichola Martin)

As 'My Camera Never Lies' fades, the drums are pushed way up in the mix as they segue into the wonderful 'Easy Love'. Take an atmospheric Giorgio Moroder era Donna Summer track as your reference point, sprinkle a little of The Fifth Dimension over the backing vocals, add a touch of Odyssey in the guitar refrain, filter the song through a British pop sensibility and place a dynamic performance from Jay Aston at the heart of it, and you have a stupendous pop song. It was one of the songs that leapt off the album as it was unlike anything the group had done before. Lyrically, it rang the changes, too; this was no broken-hearted love song, but rather it was an impassioned refusal to accept love on someone else's terms, devoid of commitment, passion or feeling. Jay is very much the star of this particular show, and this is her moment to shine, but it is worth highlighting the group's smooth harmonies that support her lead vocal beautifully, Bruce Baxter's lively brass arrangement and the subtle touches from Andy Hill, such as the synthesised train effect during the second verse that matches the lyrics.

'Easy Love' was remixed and released as a single, but only in Denmark, where it reached number 11. The song was added to the group's setlist in 1982 and was retained when the group toured in support of *Hand Cut* the following year. A flavour of how the song was performed live was captured in a stunning performance from the group's *Rhythm On Two* special in 1983. In the same year, the track was covered and released as a single by Vikki Benson, who gave the song a Hi-NRG makeover, with an Ian Levine remix of the track following in 1984.

'Love Dies Hard' (Pete Willsher/Daisy Parks)
The first of two ballads on the album. This one features an excellent lead vocal from Bobby, and although it is a track that Mike initially wanted to sing lead vocals on, there is an anguished quality to the lyrics which makes it better suited for Bobby's voice. Writing in *Record Mirror,* Daniela Soave compared this track to something The Commodores might release, and I can definitely see that, particularly on the verses and the bridge, but for me, the key to 'Love Dies Hard' is Pete Willsher. Pete, who sadly passed away in 2023, was an accomplished steel guitar player who performed with Johnny Cash, toured with Sandy Denny, recorded several albums of his own and had roots in country and folk. He not only co-wrote 'Love Dies Hard' but he also graced the song with his delicate steel guitar playing, which lends 'Love Dies Hard' a heartfelt, country ballad feel. There is a gorgeous featherlight softness to the group's harmonies on the introduction and verses, whilst Nick Ingman wraps the song in a splendid string arrangement. It could, and should, have been a *Billboard* Adult Contemporary hit at the time, if only this song and this album had been promoted across the Atlantic.

'Love Dies Hard' became part of the group's setlist during their 1982 and 1983 tours. There is a great video clip of the group performing this song during their *Rhythm On Two* special in 1983. To this day, I have no idea why Cheryl introduces Bobby in the clip as 'My Dad', but it still makes me laugh.

'One Way Love' (Andy Hill/Pete Sinfield)
A keyboard and electric guitar introduction builds anticipation for this excellent pop song with another great melody from Andy Hill. Built around that is a simple tale, eloquently told, of a man who was 'Don Juan on your day' and loved without regard for the feelings of others, who now faces a reversal of fortune, longing for someone he cannot have. There is a pop-rock edge to this track, with the electric guitars more prominent, and it always helps if you have someone of Ian Bairnson's ability to tear off a great solo

halfway through. There are strong lead vocals by the whole group throughout this song, and particularly effective is the penultimate chorus, which features the group's vocals with just drums and keyboards, then bass, before all the instrumentation returns for the final chorus.

This wasn't a single, and it was not performed on any of the group's tours in the 1980s, which is a pity as the track seems ready-made for it. Even so, this is still a fantastic pop song and one of my personal favourites.

'Are You Ready' (Andy Hill/Nichola Martin/Bucks Fizz)

In May 1982, I remember (and still have a cassette tape of) the brilliant and much missed Kenny Everett playing this track at the start of his BBC Radio 2 show and announcing, 'That's the new single from Buckets Of Fizz.' In the UK, that wasn't the case; the next single would be 'Now Those Days Are Gone' a month later, but in Germany, the Netherlands, Australia, and New Zealand, this was the single, with 'Now Those Days Are Gone' as the B-side.

The dramatic opening, enhanced by Graham Broad's clattering drums, sets the scene for an energetic song with a loosely motivational set of lyrics. It is sung by the whole group on the verses and the chorus, and it is also huge fun; perfect for starting a live show (as Bucks Fizz did on their 1982 tour) or for bouncing out of bed to and seizing the day, if that is your mood. There are some lovely, unexpected moments in the song, such as the a cappella section halfway through that gradually builds back up to the chorus. Then there is a lovely section at the end of the track where, rather than simply repeating the chorus to fade, the song is becalmed, the keyboards and drums are the main instruments, and first Bobby and Mike and then Cheryl and Jay harmonise the words of the song title and alternate lines. I have always loved this part of the song, and if someone wants to do a chilled-out, extended mix of it one day, that would be great!

The song made an unexpected return to the group's live set in the late 1980s, but, as this was not a single in the UK, very few UK fans would have seen this performed outside of a live setting. Thank heavens for the internet, which has preserved the group's appearance on the Australian show *Countdown* and their performance of the song on ZDF's *Disco* on 18 October 1982 (Episode 132), both of which were an absolute joy to discover.

'Breaking And Entering' (Andy Hill/Pete Sinfield)

Master tapes for *Are You Ready* reveal that a rough mix for 'Breaking And Entering' was completed on 6 January 1982. It is a testimony to how far and how fast Bucks Fizz had evolved that, less than a year after their formation, they are making inventive, off-the-wall pop songs like this one. The song begins with the sound of a heart beating, glass shattering and dogs barking, followed by the sound of running footsteps. The wailing police sirens in the distance get closer as the burglar's heart beats faster, and the music starts. Andy Hill's swooping bassline is the song's centre of gravity, with Graham

Broad's tremendous offbeat creating an unusual rhythm. The lyrics are sung from the intruder's point of view in a very precise way, with the first and third lines of each verse (sung by Mike and Bobby) broken into seven distinct syllables, matching the rhythm of the song. This rhythm changes for Cheryl and Jay's lines leading up to the chorus, which is sung by the whole group.

After the second chorus, the tempo changes once more, with the group's vocals weaving around some great playing by Ian Bairnson. Cheryl and Jay's vocals from the first verse are repeated, now embellished by Mike and Bobby. The final chorus is fabulous, with the group stacking one overlapping vocal harmony line on top of the other, in dizzying, thrilling and spectacular fashion, before it all comes screeching to an abrupt halt. Wonderful.

The track following this on the album undeniably highlighted the group's vocal ability, but, in a different way, so did 'Breaking And Entering'. On an album where every track could have been a single (and worldwide six of them were), this is a song that deserves greater appreciation.

'Now Those Days Are Gone' (Andy Hill/Nichola Martin)
Released as a single in June 1982. Chart place: UK: 8
An absolute gem of a song. A flawless and achingly lovely track that is beautifully written, arranged and performed, and easily one of the group's best moments. If you have never heard 'Now Those Days Are Gone', then please take four minutes out of your day to listen to this gorgeous song. The start of the track is purely a cappella and it is one minute and 13 seconds into the song before there are any instruments at all. By removing all other accompaniment, Andy Hill places the focus of the song exclusively on the group's vocals, their close four-part harmonies and Mike Nolan's exquisite lead vocal. In doing so, 'Now Those Days Are Gone' showcased the group's vocal ability in a manner that the record-buying public had not heard from them previously. Cheryl talked about creating the track on *Iain Dale's All Talk* podcast in 2021:

> Andy Hill worked out all the harmonies, and he sent us all a cassette of our individual vocal, so it was four-part harmony all the way through. I was very proud of it. It was great to record it in the studio, to hear the vocals and to use your voice like a musical instrument. It made me proud of being in the band, proud of what we could do, and it was huge, but you never hear it on the radio now.

Nichola Martin's lyrics have a poignancy to them that you appreciate more with age, whilst the strings coming in at the two-minute mark and then all quietening down again to leave just Mike's vocal in the final verse is a touch of production genius from Andy Hill. It is Bucks Fizz themselves who shine here, though, their unadorned harmonies carrying the melody and emotions of the track. The song went on to be nominated for an Ivor Novello Award in

1983 (Best Song Musically and Lyrically), ironically losing out to another Andy Hill song, 'Have You Ever Been In Love'.

'Now Those Days Are Gone' was released as a single on 11 June 1982, but only in the UK and Ireland. It was a top ten hit in both countries, reaching number eight in the UK and number five in Ireland. The 7" single came in a picture sleeve backed by a new track, 'Takin' Me Higher', and the UK also had a 7" picture disc with the same catalogue number as its standard 7" counterpart. Reviewing the single in *Record Mirror,* John Shearlaw stated that the record was 'Even more of a combination of ABBA and Chicory Tip than they've ever been, but the Fizz has been dumped in favour of a slow ballad that always threatens to take off and never actually does.' The review by future Pet Shop Boy Neil Tennant in *Smash Hits* still makes me smile: 'Soft and nostalgic with close harmonies and gentle strings. Music for crying into a freshly laundered linen handkerchief while watching a video of *The Railway Children* with the sound turned down.'

This song, along with 'Love Dies Hard', had commercial potential in North America, as did 'Easy Love', but sadly, *Are You Ready* was never released there. Instead, there was a compilation album called *Bucks Fizz* that was released with minimal promotion. 'Now Those Days Are Gone' was subsequently released as a single from this album in Canada with 'My Camera Never Lies' on the other side (RCA PB-50700), and in the US, 'Now Those Days Are Gone' became the B-side to 'The Land Of Make Believe' (RCA PB-13299).

The group appeared on *Top Of The Pops* to perform the song on 24 June 1982 (Episode 951) whilst a World War II themed promotional video, shot partially on location at Hyde Park, London, was aired on the show two weeks later on 8 July 1982 (Episode 953). In the aftermath of the group's horrendous coach crash in Newcastle in 1984, 'Now Those Days Are Gone' was included as the B-side to the group's single, 'You And Your Heart So Blue', and their first television appearance in the UK following the accident was performing this song on *The Keith Harris Show* on 18 May 1985. Later, the group performed a rerecorded version on *The Mike Yarwood Special* on 19 June 1985. By 1985, Bucks Fizz had also signed a sponsorship deal with the electronics company Sharp, which led to the group and this song appearing in a national TV commercial for Sharp compact disc players.

'Twentieth Century Hero' (Andy Hill/Pete Sinfield)

Bucks Fizz are unashamedly a pop group, with a family appeal that spreads across all age ranges – and hurrah for that by the way – but it leads to a misconception that the group's music is simplistic. Speaking to the *Boys On Film* podcast in 2020, it was a perception Jay refuted, 'There's actually a bit of prog in some of our songs in terms of the chord changes, which gave it a bit of musical magic. On the surface, it seems really poppy, but any muso will look at our music and go, 'Wow, that's a bit difficult', you know. We love that. That is what gave us a bit of an edge.' Graham Broad made a similar point in the *Percussion Discussion* podcast in 2021, 'People belittle Bucks Fizz in that era, but then we had to do the tape swaps for *Top Of The Pops,* where you have to go down and play the track. I thought I would get all these people who are (being critical of) Bucks Fizz down to do the tracks. They now had to learn it the day before, and they go, 'Bloody Hell! That's a ridiculously difficult part.' Step forward, 'Twentieth Century Hero'. On the surface, it is a bouncy little pop song that was an integral part of the group's live shows in the mid-1980s. Dig a little deeper, and there is what sounds like a 7/8 time signature, an unusual melodic sequence heading into the chorus, a fluid guitar solo from Ian Bairnson, inventive harmonies, a muted, swing-style horn section and a lyrical observation of a suburban everyman: 'You break your back from nine to five/To keep your 2.4 alive'. Not so simplistic then!

Mike and Bobby share lead vocals on the track with group harmonies on the chorus. The references to Rudolph Valentino and Errol Flynn in the lyrics, coupled with Jay and Cheryl's delightful 'You're a hero!' line leading into the chorus, which sounds like something from a 1930s RKO movie, conjures up images of the golden age of Hollywood, which, as someone who grew up with these movies and loves them to this day, is just another reason for me to like this song. Once again, these disparate elements are poured into a catchy four-minute pop song, which sees Bucks Fizz stretching out in a slightly different musical direction.

A live version of this song, recorded during the group's 1984 tour, was included on the *Talking In Your Sleep* EP. The inclusion of this live version led to a rare TV performance of the song on the BBC's *Pebble Mill At One* programme in 1984. The live version was later featured on *The Story So Far* compilation album and as the B-side to the 1989 single release of 'You Love Love'.

'Another Night' (Andy Hill/Nichola Martin)

Although 'The Land Of Make Believe' was the first single release in the UK, 'Another Night' was technically the first track to be showcased from the album. The group performed the song at The World Popular Song Festival, also known as The Yamaha Music Festival, at the Budokan Main Hall in Tokyo, Japan, on Sunday 1 November 1981, and ended up being awarded a grand prize. TV coverage of the show was shown on Fuji TV (4 November 1981) and Japan TV (14 November 1981) in addition to radio broadcasts via the Nippon Broadcasting System. TV footage of the group's performance from the show currently exists online. As a result, this song was released as a single, but only in Japan (RCA RPS 52) and came with a unique picture insert and 'Took It To The Limit' on the B-side.

Musically, it is the closest in style to the group's debut album and compared to tracks such as 'Breaking And Entering' and 'My Camera Never Lies', it sounds like one of the earlier tracks written for the album. Bobby and Mike are on lead vocals, trading lines with Cheryl and Jay leading up to the chorus, which is sung by the whole group. Andy Hill's (uncredited) backing vocals on the 'one more heart attack' section and continuing through the key change and into the final chorus are also a standout moment. Despite being a happy-sounding song with a catchy sing-along chorus, the lyrics at the start of each verse are actually quite forlorn: 'Long time gone/Just sitting here wondering why I carry on' and 'Tears will fall/Looking back on life it seems I've done it all'. The song takes the idea of missing someone who you know is never coming back to you and going out for the evening to lose yourself and forget these feelings. The lyrics in the chorus state 'Another night like this/And I'll be heading for the town/Another night like this/And there'll be action going down', implying an evening pursuing pleasure or excitement as a diversion. In 2008, an alternate version with different lyrics in the chorus was unearthed on *Lost Masters 2* that pushed this idea a little further. On this version, the lyrics are 'Another night like this/Will put me six feet underground/Another night when you're not here/To stop me falling down', suggesting something closer to a night of excess and a loss of control without the other person's restraining influence.

'The Land Of Make Believe' (Andy Hill/Pete Sinfield)
Released as a single in November 1981. Chart place: UK: 1
On first listen, 'The Land Of Make Believe' is a happy, harmless, fun pop song, a children's song really, and if that is what you want it to be, then that's what it is for you. For those who loved 'The Land Of Make Believe' at the time of its release, the ensuing four decades have imbued the song with nostalgia, transporting the listener back to their younger days. Pete Sinfield's evocative lyrics recall childhood innocence, fantasy, adventure and escapism, but they also contain some disquieting images – intentionally so by the lyricist's own admission – which leaves the song open to alternative, disconcerting lyrical interpretations upon closer examination.

There is a fairy tale-like quality to the song, and the opening lines, sung by Bobby, are perfect: 'Stars in your eyes, little one/Where do you go to dream/To a place, we all know/The Land Of Make Believe'. It builds up anticipation for what is to follow, like a 'Once upon a time' in a story book, before the melody bursts out of the speakers and the musical adventure begins. These opening lines also borrow an idea from J.M. Barrie's *Peter Pan* of the Neverland being a liminal space between waking and sleeping.

Pete Sinfield's lyrics in the first verse have an unsettling quality: 'Shadows tapping at your window/Ghostly voices whisper will you come and play'. The lyrics may seem odd, but fairy tales have never been purely harmless escapism. These stories appeal to the imagination, intellect and emotions, and part of their potency lies not only in being enchanting stories, but also in giving substance to formless, nameless fears (think of the Wicked Queen in *Snow White* or the wolf in *Little Red Riding Hood,* for example) that are ultimately transcended or defeated. In the lines that follow, the disembodied voices are shrugged off in an almost childlike way, 'Not for all the tea in

China/All the corn in Carolina'. *Smash Hits* may have branded these lyrics as 'pathetic', but not surprisingly, I disagree. Pete Sinfield was a superb lyricist and not someone inclined to write something without thought or care. For me, his lyrics capture all of what fairy tales are: their magic, wonder, enchantment, excitement, adventure and naivete, as well as their underlying menace.

In an interview with *Modern Dance,* Pete Sinfield also claimed that the song contained heavily veiled political references: 'It is ten times more difficult to write a 3+ minute hit song with a veneer of integrity than it is to write anything for King Crimson or ELP. But I half succeeded. For instance, 'The Land Of Make Believe', beneath its 'tra-la-las', is a virulent anti-Thatcher song. Oh yes, it is! 'Something nasty in your garden, waiting, till it can steal your heart'. Lovely, and my first number one.' In Andrew Gibson's excellent, thought-provoking analysis, the 'something nasty' is, 'In Sinfield's framing … the seductive pull of Thatcherite ideology, infiltrating the private spaces of the British psyche – your home, your garden, your child's imagination'. Some of the lyrics are chilling when viewed in this context. It is a reminder that pop does not always equal disposable, and rebellion is not always righteous anger and guitars. If you believe that 'The Land Of Make Believe' is a subversive protest song, then it can be that for you, too.

Musically, the song was a giant leap forward from the first album. Andy Hill's production positively sparkles, and beneath its memorable hookline lies a reggae rhythm that allows Graham Broad to cut loose during the middle eight and the final third of the song. Offsetting the darker elements in the lyrics, it is a happy, sunny, vibrant track. The two-boy, two-girl vocals in the verses are beautifully executed with exuberant group harmonies in the chorus. One effective part of the song, though, was the result of an accident, as Brian Tench told *International Musician And Recording World* in 1985:

> I remember Bobby had to drive all the way down from Manchester, where the band were staying, to do some vocals and then drive all the way back for the show the same night. We spent all day overdubbing his voice and bouncing it together to make a six-part harmony thing on the middle eight. He did it all, and he'd got back in the car and was only half a mile down the road when Andy and I started to clean up the track and just when we got to the parts he'd been doing on the words 'far away'. I don't know what happened, but I pressed the button early and erased the lot! You should have seen Andy's face. He went white, stood up and walked out without a word. I searched all over the multitrack, and I found one place where I'd left the very original voice. So, I smothered it in echo and reverb and made it sound like it was miles away and set in amongst the big block harmonies, which were on the vocals on the rest of the song.

The inventive fade out of the song features a nursery rhyme, also written by Pete Sinfield, which was narrated by 11-year-old Abby Kimber, daughter of

RCA executive Bill Kimber: 'I've got a friend that comes to tea/And no one else can see, but me/He came today, but had to go/To visit you? You never know'. I have heard some people remark that they find this part of the song unnerving, even chilling, but equally, this visitation could be the start of the most thrilling and fantastical adventure that you have ever been on, in an enchanted place unique to you: your own Land of Make Believe.

There was a magical quality to the promotional video, too, which was filmed at White City swimming baths in London. It begins in black and white with Cheryl asleep in bed (she would later joke, 'It's weird. I'm in bed, but I've got a mac on! What's all that about?') before being transported *Wizard Of Oz* style to a world of colour. There are a few references to *Cinderella* and *The Lion, The Witch And The Wardrobe* as Cheryl's outfit is miraculously transformed before she makes her way through the trees and the crowd to join the rest of the group who are waiting for her. Jay's innate flair for fashion comes to the fore from this single onwards as she creates the group's look. Cheryl and Jay both look gorgeous in outfits from Kahn and Bell, whilst Mike and Bobby adopt a fetching, almost punk look from Boy. The original video has a slightly different mix on the vocals in the second verse, which can be heard on the *Very Best Of Bucks Fizz* DVD, but this version also edits Jay's raunchy 'come to sunny Florida' section seen on the *Greatest Hits* VHS video.

The group first performed the song on *Top Of The Pops* on 10 December 1981 (Episode 922), with the record at number 24. The Christmas chart was announced on Tuesday 22 December, with Human League at number one with 'Don't You Want Me' and Bucks Fizz at number five. The group appeared on *Top Of The Pops* on Christmas Eve 1981 (Episode 924), and Bucks Fizz finally ascended to the top of the charts on 12 January 1982, with the group returning to *Top Of The Pops* on 14 January 1982 (Episode 928) to perform the song. Their pre-Christmas performance repeated on 21 January 1982 (Episode 929) when the group held on to the number one slot for a second week.

Mike Nolan famously had doubts about the single's potential, but it went on to become a number one in Belgium, Ireland and the Netherlands and a top 20 hit in Australia, Austria, Denmark, Israel and Germany. It also became the group's biggest-selling single in the UK and saw the group return for the Christmas Day edition of *Top Of The Pops* in 1982 (Episode 978), which has a special place in my heart. It featured the entire group in pantomime-style fancy dress, made especially by the BBC costume department, with Bobby as a flamboyant pantomime dame complete with a head dress and Cheryl in a beautiful fairy costume suspended on wires, who takes flight during the dance routine. How can you not love a group that does this?

In the UK, there was no 12" single, but there was one in Germany (RCA Victor PC5471), which included 'Midnight Reservation' as a bonus track. Japan had a promotional 12" (RCA SPLD 1174), which had a unique sleeve and included a Christmas greeting from the band members at the start of the track. The UK had two 7" versions, a standard one with a picture sleeve and a limited edition with a festive outer sleeve and a 7" by 35" poster depicting scenes from the video. The single was released in multiple countries, but the most interesting variations are the Japanese 7" (RCA RPS 89) and US one (PB 13299), both of which featured different picture sleeves and 'Now Those Days Are Gone' on the B-side. Seven-inch singles from Mexico, Panama and El Salvador (again on red vinyl) include an edited version of 'Siento Soledades', the Spanish language version of 'Getting Kinda Lonely', on the B-side.

There have been other versions of the song over the years. All Stars took their version to number nine in UK in 2002, Celine Dion recorded her French language version, 'A Quatre Pas D'ici', for her 1983 compilation album *Du Soleil Au Coeur,* French singer Sheila (of Sheila and B. Devotion fame) recorded a version with totally different lyrics entitled 'Condition Feminine' and Brazilian girl group Harmony Cats released their version 'A Terra Do Faz De Conta' on their self-titled third album, which went gold in their native country. It was another of the group's songs nominated for an Ivor Novello Award (Best Song Musically and Lyrically) in 1982.

'The Land Of Make Believe' has always felt like a Christmas song in spirit, and in a perfect world, it would have topped the charts a few weeks earlier, been a deserved Christmas number one and been included on festive compilation albums ever since. Whatever your interpretation of the song, I have lost count of the number of times that someone has told me, or I have read, that this song provided an escape for them from a difficult situation at the time, or transports them back to a happier time in their life. For me, it is both. That's what this song does, and that is part of the enduring magic of 'The Land Of Make Believe'.

Related Tracks

Eight original tracks were added to the 2015 *Are You Ready: The Definitive Edition* CD.

'Now You're Gone' (Andy Hill/Nichola Martin)

Originally the B-side to 'Land Of Make Believe' and the group's only Christmas track. It is an affecting song with a heart-meltingly gorgeous lead vocal by Cheryl Baker. This has always felt like an end-of-the-evening song, a gentle keyboard-led ballad reflecting on a relationship that did not turn out as envisaged, yet the sentiment of missing someone at Christmas is broad enough to encompass friends or family members, too. On *Lost Masters 2,* there is an uncredited bonus track on disc one, displayed on streaming sites as 'It Doesn't Feel Like Christmas (Deleted End Section)', that reveals another direction the end of this song could have taken with a variation to the melody line and group harmonies in preference to Cheryl's solo vocal.

'What Am I Gonna Do' (Daisy Parks/Bill Edwards)

Written by Daisy Parks, who co-wrote 'Love Dies Hard', and Bill Edwards, who would later receive a co-write credit on '10, 9, 8, 7, 6, 5, 4' from *Hand*

Cut. This track originally appeared on the B-side of 'My Camera Never Lies', and it is an unusual one. The verses are a lovers' quarrel via telephone between an errant and repentant Bobby, and Jay, who, although hurt by Bobby's actions, still forgives him before adding that it will be 'the first and the last time I'll do it/The next time I'll help you pack'. The keyboard sound is a little reminiscent of PhD's song 'I Won't Let You Down', which had been a hit in Australia in late 1981 prior to achieving similar success in the UK charts in 1982, whilst Jay and Bobby's vocals in the hookline of this song have a somewhat abrasive quality, described by Bob Stanley in *The Guardian* as 'a growled chorus' that was uncharacteristic of Bucks Fizz at that time.

'My Camera Never Lies (12" Version)' (Andy Hill/Nichola Martin)
Although there would be many remixes of this track in the decades to come, this was the group's first-ever extended 12" mix from 1982. It mirrors the 7" mix until 2.21, when the chorus is broken down to just the beat and Cheryl and Jay's vocals. The song is then gradually built back up with the keyboards added, then the bass, and finally the guitars. The 12" has a longer fade out than its 7" counterpart, and if you listen carefully at the end of the track, you can hear Graham Broad's distinctive drum fill that was pushed up in the mix on the album version to become the start of 'Easy Love'.

'Takin' Me Higher' (Bucks Fizz)
Originally the B-side to 'Now Those Days Are Gone'. This was the first song written and produced by the group themselves, and an excellent one it is, too, arguably their strongest B-side up to this point. The rattling rhythm and overlapping harmony vocals in the verses, with Cheryl particularly prominent, are fabulous and the highlight of the song for me. The chorus sounds like it belongs to another song entirely, not only due to a change in rhythm and tempo but also as it shifts lyrically from third person observation in the verses ('You thought you'd never lose/When you were wrong from the start') to a first person declaration that 'Your loving is taking me higher'. It's difficult to see how these two parts fit together, but somehow it all seems to work, and any lingering doubts are obliterated by a thrilling solo vocal by Jay towards the end.

'Another Night (Alternate Version)' (Andy Hill/Nichola Martin)
A different vocal take of the song, first released on *Lost Masters 2* in 2008, with an alternative set of lyrics for the chorus. If the lyrics of the album version suggest an evening of escapism, then the lyrics of this alternate version sound more like a night of excess: 'Another night like this/Will put me six feet underground/Another night when you're not here/ To stop me falling down'. The group had a lot of young fans, particularly at this point in their career, so I can see why this set of lyrics was not used, but this version still makes me smile each time I hear it.

'Another Night (Yamaha Song Contest Live Version)' (Andy Hill/ Nicola Martin)
The World Popular Song Festival was held 20 times between 1970 and 1989, with Bucks Fizz performing in November 1981. This live performance was originally only available on a Japanese compilation album on Yamaha's own label in 1981. The album featured performances from 12 contestants and was housed in a gatefold sleeve with a photo book and a musical score insert.

'My Camera Never Lies (Dead Ending Version)' (Andy Hill/Nichola Martin)
A dead-ending mix that was sometimes used for TV performances. This mix was one of several dead-end versions that appeared on *The Very Best Of Bucks Fizz,* in preference to the original 7" versions.

'Easy Love (European Version)' (Andy Hill/Nichola Martin)
The record label states 'Made In Germany', but this remixed single version appears to have only been released in Denmark, which is the copy I have (RCA Victor PB 68006). This mix features more reverb on the lead and backing vocals, giving it a spacious feel, and the brass section is a little more prominent. It is nice to hear as a variation, but the album version remains definitive and best.

Two further original tracks appeared on *The Lost Masters*:

'Easy Love (Blazer's Version)' (Andy Hill/Nichola Martin)
An edited, mono mix of the track with a dead ending, produced for the *Rhythm On Two* TV Special. The track is edited at the start and after the second chorus to shorten the track from 5.01 to 3.39.

'Breaking And Entering (Demo)' (Andy Hill/Pete Sinfield)
Omitting all the sound effects at the start of the finished album track, this version consists of the main body of the song preceded by a count-in from Andy Hill. What remains is a surprisingly sophisticated demo with most of the harmony lines intact but fading out at the end rather than arriving at a dead ending as the finished track does.

An additional track appeared on *The Lost Masters 2 – The Final Cut*:

'My Camera Never Lies (Alternate Mix)' (Andy Hill/Nichola Martin)
Not a radical departure, but it includes a vocal line from Mike and Bobby at the 2.40 mark that was cut from the album version. The most significant difference is the end section, which is slightly longer and includes two overdubs of Jay's spoken word 'my camera has good eyes' line and variations of the 'my cam-er-a' hook that appeared earlier in the song. On a related

point, the group's performance on *Razzmatazz* on 12 March 1982 features a hitherto unreleased mix of this song with fewer harmonies and keyboards, omitting Jay's spoken part entirely but including Mike and Bobby's missing additional line from this mix.

Hand Cut (1983)

Personnel:
Mike Nolan: lead vocals, backing vocals
Cheryl Baker: lead vocals, backing vocals
Bobby G: lead vocals, backing vocals
Jay Aston: lead vocals, backing vocals
Andy Hill: keyboards, bass, guitars
Graham Broad: drums and percussion
Ian Bairnson: guitars
Nichola Martin: keyboards
Richard Cottle: keyboards
Pete Wingfield: keyboards
John Read: bass
Chris Hunter: saxophone
Spike: trombone
Guy Barker: trumpet
Anne Dudley: string arrangements
Recorded at Mayfair Studios, London; Utopia Studios, London; Power Plant, London; RG Jones Studio, Wimbledon; Comforts Place, Surrey, between 1982 and 1983
Producer: Andy Hill, Brian Tench and Bobby G
Engineers: Brian Tench, Martin Webster, John Hudson
Original sleeve concept and photography: John Thornton
Design and art direction: Andrew Christian
Inner sleeve photography: Gerard Mankowitz
UK release date: March 1983
Charts: UK: 17

The *Hand Cut* era began in earnest in November 1982 with the announcement of a UK tour during March and April 1983 and a new single: 'If You Can't Stand The Heat'. Prior to that, though, Bucks Fizz found themselves at the Theatre Royal, Drury Lane, London, on 8 November 1982, participating in the Royal Variety Performance in the presence of Her Majesty Queen Elizabeth the Queen Mother. After two previous royal shows that year, one for children and the other for the Falklands Task Force's National Salute, the decision was taken to make musicals the theme of the show. As a result, the group performed 'You'll Never Walk Alone' from *Carousel*. The show was broadcast on 14 November 1982.

'If You Can't Stand The Heat' became the group's fourth consecutive top ten hit, and in addition to TV appearances throughout November and December to promote the single, the group were guests on *Saturday Superstore* on 20 November 1982 and appeared on *Des O'Connor Tonight* two days later to perform 'The Land Of Make Believe' and join the host on a rendition of the Diana Ross song 'Old Funky Rolls'. December also saw the group on the

Christmas Day edition of *Top Of The Pops* for a gloriously silly performance of 'The Land Of Make Believe', release a flexi disc (a studio version of their Live Medley) via *Flexipop* magazine and issue their first official wall calendar, which my best friend and I spent several days that month attempting to track down.

After the success of *Are You Ready,* the expectation might have been for Bucks Fizz to attempt to replicate this by offering more of the same with the same team of writers, but that is not what happened on *Hand Cut*. For the previous album, Andy Hill had collaborated with Nichola Martin or Pete Sinfield on nine of the ten tracks, but only one track on this album bore that credit ('Shot Me Through The Heart'); instead, Andy Hill wrote with guitarists Ian Bairnson and Alan Coates or wrote the lyrics himself. Steve Glen (who had co-written 'One Of Those Nights') returned with another song that he had co-written ('10, 9, 8, 7, 6, 5, 4') whilst Bobby G contributed the first song written by an individual member of the group ('Surrender Your Heart'). The group secured an excellent original song by Andy Sells ('You Love, Love') whilst 'I'd Like To Say I Love You' was the first of several songs penned by Warren Harry (a.k.a. Warren Bacall), who would become one of the principal songwriters for Bucks Fizz for the remainder of 1983.

Musically, *Hand Cut* was an evolution rather than a revolution. The up-tempo tracks saw Bucks Fizz jettison many of their remaining M.O.R elements and fully embrace a contemporary pop sound. Andy Hill's production style from mid-1982 and throughout 1983 displayed a penchant for complex, overlapping harmony lines and a huge drum sound, and both of these are present on *Hand Cut*. The inventive percussion of Graham Broad, that was used to good effect on tracks such as 'My Camera Never Lies', 'The Land Of Make Believe' and 'Easy Love', is much more prevalent on this album and integral to tracks such as 'Run For Your Life' or '10, 9, 8, 7, 6, 5, 4'. Although *Are You Ready* contained three tracks with solo vocals, the remaining songs on the album featured male and female vocals singing alternating lines, and whilst that pattern continues on *Hand Cut*, the way the group's vocals are used on several tracks starts to diversify. Bobby has two lead vocals on this album, but for 'I'd Like To Say I Love You', he shares it with Jay, who sings the bridge. Jay also has two lead vocals on this album, but the second of these, 'Running Out Of Time', contains overlapping vocal harmonies by the group from the second verse onwards, making it feel like an ensemble piece as much as a solo number by Jay. Even casual fans who only knew Bucks Fizz through their singles would have noticed a change in the group's sound with the album's lead single, 'If You Can't Stand The Heat', which featured electric guitars more prominently, and was the first Bucks Fizz single to feature a brass section in addition to being the first Bucks Fizz track to showcase Cheryl and Jay as joint lead vocalists.

The release of *Hand Cut* was preceded by a trip to Chile to perform two sets at Festival Internacional de la Canción de Viña del Mar on 13 and 14 February. This was followed by a UK tour, to which further dates had been added, starting on 3 March 1983 and consisting of 39 shows in 47 days, although a handful of these dates would be cancelled when Bobby G fell ill.

Smash Hits were quite complimentary and awarded the album 7 out of 10. *Record Mirror* gave the album two stars and remarked, 'Time was when you could rely on Bucks Fizz to put a stamp of class on lightweight pop, but now … Bucks Fizz are devaluing themselves. What happened to those once stunning harmony lines? Perhaps they think they don't have to try anymore?' Commercially, the album fell a little short of expectations; 'Run For Your Life' peaked at number 14, breaking a sequence of top ten singles, and although *Hand Cut* earned a silver disc, it peaked at number 17, the group's lowest-charting album so far. The decision was taken not to release further singles from *Hand Cut,* which, in hindsight, is a pity as the album contained several tracks worthy of release as a single. Some vinyl copies of *Hand Cut* featured a sticker on the cover highlighting the inclusion of '10, 9, 8, 7, 6, 5, 4', which suggests this track may have been considered as a single at some point. For the two preceding Bucks Fizz albums, a ballad had been released as the third single, which would point to the two ballads on *Hand Cut*, 'You Love Love' or 'Where The Ending Starts' as the follow-up to 'Run For Your Life'. However, my personal choice would have been 'I'd Like To Say I Love You', which I think would have made a fine single in the summer of 1983.

Original vinyl copies of the album in 1983 came with an inner sleeve, which featured a beautiful picture of the group (taken by Gerard Mankowitz), with the album credits on one side and the lyrics on the other. Worth looking out for is the Australian vinyl edition, containing the same information but as a gatefold sleeve. Twenty-one years later, *Hand Cut* was released on CD with six bonus tracks (plus a hidden extra one), and in 2015, it was issued as a 2CD edition which incorporated a second disc of 'Post *Hand Cut* Material'. At the time of the album, Bucks Fizz filmed a *Rhythm On 2* TV special at Blazers, Windsor. The show was bookended by the two singles and included performances of 'I'd Like To Say I Love You' and 'You Love, Love', two rare TV performances of 'Love Dies Hard' and 'Easy Love', plus 'My Camera Never Lies' from *Are You Ready* and featured Andy Hill and Nichola Martin's group Paris as special guests. It beautifully captures Bucks Fizz as they were at the time of *Hand Cut,* but by the time it was aired in July 1983, the group had released 'When We Were Young' a month earlier, were working on a new album and were already heading somewhere else with their music.

Hand Cut may not have a number one single as a calling card like its predecessors, but it is a record I have tremendous affection for. Primarily, that is due to a collection of great pop songs that I have loved for over 40 years, the warmth of Andy Hill's production, the tremendous drum sound, the group's vocals and the inventive arrangements and harmonies. For me, it is also an album bathed in the glow of teenage nostalgia. Some albums just make you feel better when you play them, and for me, *Hand Cut* is one of them.

'Run For Your Life' (Andy Hill/Ian Bairnson)

Released as a single in March 1983. Chart place: UK: 14

Released just ahead of the album and a UK tour starting at Edinburgh Playhouse on 3 March 1983, 'Run For Your Life' was the second single from the album and the highest new entry at number 31 when the singles chart was announced on Radio 1 at lunchtime on Tuesday 8 March: Cheryl Baker's birthday! It went on to become the group's eighth consecutive top 20 hit, peaking at number 14, and a top ten hit in Ireland, where it reached number eight. As a teenager, I devoured this single, and I loved everything about it: the song, the production, the picture sleeve, the video and the look the group adopted for their TV appearances. It is a fantastic pop song and a perfect opening track for the album.

This was the second single written by Andy Hill and Ian Bairnson, and although it is a different type of song from 'If You Can't Stand The Heat', it also seems to be built around a phrase and a guitar riff. Mike and Bobby share joint lead vocals on the verses, trading alternate lines with Cheryl and Jay on the bridge before the whole group sing the chorus. There is an imaginative use of vocals throughout this track; listen out for the two separate vocal melody lines between the first chorus and the second verse, or the variations to this between the second chorus and the middle eight, which features wonderful harmonies from Cheryl and Jay. Another standout moment is at 3.22 when the group sing 'The shadow won't be far behind in the heat of the night', collectively holding the note on the final word, whilst Cheryl and Jay's wordless harmonies provide a complementary melody line alongside that.

The group performed this track on *Top Of The Pops* on 17 March 1983 (Episode 990) as well as on the prime-time Saturday evening show *Paul Squire Esq* on 2 April 1983 and *Saturday Superstore* on 26 February 1983. The track had a paranormal-themed promotional video set in a deserted manor house. Starting at the second verse, there is a sequence during which the group perform the song to a camera, beginning with the group entering a mist-filled and brightly lit white room. This room is completely empty with the exception of four plinths with a marble bust situated on top of each one. Each member of the group approaches one of these plinths and circles clockwise around it. Thematically, this image ties in with John Thornton's concept for the *Hand Cut* album cover, which depicts each member of the group as a sculpted marble bust, individually mounted on separate plinths and presented like idealised Greco-Roman statues in a temple. The 'Run For Your Life' theme extends to the single sleeve, which depicts the group running away from molten lava, with an erupting volcano in the background. The UK also had a limited edition 10" picture disc which used the same image. Most international sleeves are variations on the UK version, but it is worth seeking out the Spanish promo copy (RCA Victor ESP-602), which replicates the *Hand Cut* album sleeve and features 'If You Can't Stand The Heat' on the B-side.

Ian Birch in *Smash Hits* made a valid point that the song was too cluttered and had no room to breathe, whilst Robin Smith, writing in *Record Mirror* on 5 March 1983, declared, 'This is a bit desperate. These days, the Hill/Martin partnership seems to be aiming at producing as many varieties of 'My Camera Never Lies' as they possibly can.' For me, though, 'Run For Your Life' was, and still is, an excellent pop song with a great production. The first two singles had made me excited to hear what the rest of the album would hold. I thought that *Hand Cut* could turn out to be something really special.

'10, 9, 8, 7, 6, 5, 4' (Steve Glen/Matthew James/Bill Edwards)
This track marked the first appearance of Brian Tench as a producer for Bucks Fizz, in collaboration with Bobby G. Brian Tench went into Mayfair Studios straight out of school in 1975, expecting to spend the summer working there before going to University. Instead, he remained there for the next eight years, working first as a tape operator and later as an engineer alongside studio owner John Hudson. He worked with Andy Hill on the *Are You Ready* album, and by the time *Hand Cut* was released, he had signed to Big Note as a record producer in his own right and was starting to make a name for himself with credits including 'Go Wild In The Country' for Bow Wow Wow and 'Iko Iko' for The Belle Stars. Just three months after the release of *Hand Cut,* Brian Tench would co-produce 'When We Were Young' with Andy Hill, helping give Bucks Fizz a heavier sound. On the group's next album, *I Hear Talk,* his solo productions would adopt a more keyboard-oriented approach, perhaps lacking the warmth of Andy Hill's productions but entirely appropriate for darker, foreboding Bucks Fizz songs such as 'Thief In The Night'. For now, though, the tracks he co-produced with Bobby G on *Hand Cut* remained faithful to Andy Hill's style and '10, 9, 8, 7, 6, 5, 4' fits in seamlessly with the rest of the album.

This is another excellent track with its buoyant rhythm, bright keyboards, funky bassline and superb, inventive percussion from Graham Broad, which undeniably enhances the track. The group themselves bring a lot to the song, too, with imaginative harmonies throughout the second verse, chorus and bridge. The final chorus repeats twice, but in the last 40 seconds, the track goes spinning off with a flurry of drums, an unanticipated key change and the introduction of a new melody with the 'We've been through this, we've said it all before' lines, sung by Jay and Cheryl. It is interesting to contrast the Bucks Fizz version with a later one by fellow Eurovision winners Herreys, who covered it on their 1985 album *Crazy People.* Stripped of the percussive elements and not even attempting the complex harmonies, the song sounds a bit pedestrian by comparison.

The composers included two people who had written for Bucks Fizz before: Steve Glen ('One Of Those Nights') and Bill Edwards ('What Am I Gonna Do'), and the track featured in the setlist for the group's 1983 tour, sandwiched between 'Love Dies Hard' and 'Easy Love'.

'I Do It All For You' (Andy Hill/Alan Coates)
The only Bucks Fizz song to feature a co-write credit from Alan Coates. *Hand Cut* is by no means an angst-ridden album, but the lyrics of several tracks portray relationships that are not working out ('Where The Ending Starts', 'Shot Me Through The Heart', 'You Love, Love', 'I'd Like To Say I Love You'). Alan Coates' lyrics here are a refreshing contrast to all of that, as they express how love for another person is the inspiration and motivation behind all that they do, and it provides the album's one unashamedly positive romantic moment. In addition to formerly being a member of Prima Donna with Jay's elder brother, Lance Aston, and later a member of The Hollies with Cheryl's future husband, Steve Stroud, Alan was the guitar player in Bucks Fizz's touring band at the time of this album's release. If you have a rainy afternoon free, I invite you to explore the histories of bands such as Screemer, Sprinkler, Filmstars, M Squad, Sparrow and Beyond, as well as reading Tom Marshall's excellent book, *Catch A Falling Star,* to get an idea of the myriad connections between the musicians that formed such an integral part of the Bucks Fizz story.

'I Do It All For You' was another of the songs Bucks Fizz included in their setlist during their 1983 tour, and it is a fabulous pop song with a euphoric hook line and a sophisticated production that resists the temptation to embellish too much and simply allows the gorgeous melodies and harmonies to flourish. Bobby's voice dominates in the opening lines, with Cheryl adding subtle touches as she softly sings the same lines in unison. The whole group join in as we head towards the song's marvellous chorus, with Mike and Bobby to the fore and Jay and Cheryl adding some delightful harmonies, especially during their own lines at the end.

Following the second chorus, there is a bridge section, where the male and female vocals alternate in a distinctly ABBA-esque fashion, culminating in the lines 'When you give me love I can't let go'. At this point, the song takes flight, with a key change and a brief guitar solo from Ian Bairnson. As his solo recedes, the chorus returns once more, but this time only the opening lyrics of the chorus are sung ('My love, I do it all for you, my love.../My love, I do it all for you'). These two lines are repeated twice, and the group's cascading harmonies on the words 'I do it all for you', occurring on the second and fourth lines, are simply glorious. The two lines are repeated for a third and final time before the song calms and fades gently into 'Where The Ending Starts'. 'I Do It All For You' is a thoroughly ravishing piece of pop music. It is one of my strongest memories of the 1983 tour and one of the many highlights of *Hand Cut.*

'Where The Ending Starts' (Andy Hill)
Fading in at the end of 'I Do It All For You' is this gentle ballad, with Jay delivering a touching lead vocal, sung from the perspective of a woman still very much in love, but reflecting on a relationship that has gradually become

distant and may have run its course. Anne Dudley, fresh from her recent work on ABC's magnificent debut album *The Lexicon Of Love,* wraps the song in another wonderful string arrangement whilst Chris Hunter adds a fine saxophone solo. These two elements combine with gorgeous harmonies from the group at the song's conclusion. It is a beautifully constructed song, and for someone who once claimed that he didn't like writing lyrics and found it to be hard work, Andy Hill expresses the emotions succinctly here, and Jay conveys them with tenderness and feeling.

Although I am firmly of the opinion that if a third single were taken from *Hand Cut,* it simply had to be 'I'd Like To Say I Love You', there are those who would argue that RCA missed a trick in not releasing this track as a single in 1983. In fairness, they may have a point, as negative and positive reviews alike called attention to it, with Ian Birch in his review of the album in *Smash Hits* arguing that 'the best songs are the slower and less complicated ones – like 'Where The Ending Starts'.' The track did make it to 7" vinyl, but only as a B-side, when it partnered the group's next single, the startlingly different 'When We Were Young'.

'Surrender Your Heart' (Bobby G)

The second of two tracks co-produced by Brian Tench also featured a significant contribution from Bobby, who co-produced the track with him and wrote the song. Vocally, however, it is Mike who takes centre stage. Although Bucks Fizz were built around him, Mike received comparatively few solo lead vocals, which is a shame, as the ones he did were all excellent. This track is no exception, with Bobby taking a back seat vocally and Cheryl and Jay providing the majority of the supporting harmonies. The soft keyboards of the introduction and Mike's melodic vocal lighten the mood after Jay's emotional 'Where The Ending Starts', whilst a happy, memorable chorus, which belies the lyrics a little ('You know I'd do anything/But I'm in the dark'), provides an excellent way to close out 'side one'. Time for a brief pause before turning the album over, where more fabulous pop songs and a couple of the group's best moments await.

'If You Can't Stand The Heat' (Andy Hill/Ian Bairnson)

Released as a single in November 1982. Chart place: UK: 10

'If You Can't Stand The Heat' was released in November 1982 and was the lead single from the album. It became the group's fifth top ten single and their seventh consecutive top 20 hit, earning the group a silver disc for sales of over 250,000 in the UK.

Although he had been the guitarist on their two previous albums, this was the first Bucks Fizz track to carry a co-write credit for Ian Bairnson (1953-2023). Ian was born in Lerwick in Shetland and joined the group Pilot in 1974, lending his distinctive playing to their enduring pop classics 'Magic' and 'January'. The first two Pilot albums, and their underrated fourth, *Two's A*

Crowd, were produced by Alan Parsons, which led to Ian becoming an integral part of the Alan Parsons Project and gracing all of their albums with his exceptional playing. He also played on Kate Bush's first four albums, with his glorious guitar solo appearing at the close of Kate's iconic debut single 'Wuthering Heights'. On Ian's passing in 2023, Alan Parsons described him as 'a musical genius', adding, 'He was a true master of the guitar – he knew every possible playable guitar chord and how to describe it.'

Never content to release the same record twice, the single was another departure for Bucks Fizz, with a slight reggae rhythm underpinning the track, a riff that dictates the direction of the melody, a prominent brass section and Cheryl and Jay sharing a joint lead vocal for the first time. Andy Hill observed in a 1983 interview on Radio One:

> It was mainly a song written around an idea. I think it was a US President (Harry S Truman) and this famous phrase he had, 'If you can't stand the heat, keep out of the kitchen' … With that song, I think the hook line was the mainstay of it, and everything else, and the lyrics, were something building up to the hook line.

The promotional video depicted an imaginary 'day in the life of Bucks Fizz', beginning with an oversleeping Jay Aston, followed by rehearsals, soundcheck and press interviews, culminating in a performance of the song at the Shaftesbury Theatre in London. The group performed the song on *Top Of The Pops* twice. The first appearance was on 2 December 1982 (Episode 974), with the clip repeated two weeks later when the single entered the top 20. A second performance was shown on 6 January 1983 (Episode 980), and the group also performed the song on *Crackerjack* (17 December), *Razzmatazz, The Keith Harris Show* (31 December) and a number of TV Shows in Europe. All of these appearances featured a distinctive look, fashioned by Jay, who accessorised the group's outfits using chamois leathers and mop heads.

For Bucks Fizz collectors, there were lots of different variations of the single to look out for. The 7" single came in two different sleeves, yellow and orange (RCA 300), in addition to one with a poster sleeve and a 7" picture disc (RCA P 300) featuring a stunning picture of the group, which was also used as the cover of their 1983 calendar. There was also a 12" single (RCAT 300), featuring an extended version of the A-side. All variations featured a new track, 'Stepping Out', as the B-side.

'I'd Like To Say I Love You' (Warren Harry)

Warren Harry (1953-2008), also known as Warren Bacall, was someone who would feature prominently in the songwriting credits for Bucks Fizz throughout 1983 and 1984. In the 1970s, Warren performed with his band, The Yum Yum Band, and released several singles as Warren Harry in the UK and Northern Europe. These were: 'I Don't Care' (1976), 'I Am A Radio' (1977), 'Sail On' (1977), '1965' (1978), 'Radio Show' (1979) and 'Welcome To Judy's World' (1980). He released a further single, 'Lions And Tigers', under the name Warren Bacall in 1982, and later two Andy Hill-produced singles, 'Brief Encounter' and 'Crystal Tears', in 1984. His solo work exists beyond the realms of streaming sites or even compact discs, but a YouTube search brings up a wealth of material for those who want to investigate further.

This was the first of his songs to be recorded by Bucks Fizz, and what an utterly magnificent one it is. A galloping keyboard rhythm introduces the song, which tells a story of a relationship that is compassionate but devoid of the spark of genuine love at its core. Bobby delivers a fine vocal in the verses, the group join in on the song's killer hook line, and then, just when you think this song cannot get any better, it does. Following the second chorus, there is a soaring solo vocal by Jay before the song lifts again, changing key, going back into the chorus once more, with Anne Dudley's string arrangement supplying the ideal finishing touch. Little wonder that the group chose this song to open the show on their 1983 tour. It is one of the group's finest moments and came top of a poll on the Bucks Fizz Early Years website in 2004 as the group's best song. 'I'd Like To Say I Love You' is pop perfection – and don't let anyone tell you otherwise.

Although the song was not released as a single, it featured on a *Rhythm On 2* TV special filmed at Blazers Nightclub in Windsor and first broadcast on BBC2 on 30 July 1983. Prior to that, on 26 February 1983, there was an unusual first performance of the song on *Saturday Superstore.* Following their return from Chile, the group were due to be on the island of Jersey for the show. In the event, only Cheryl and Bobby made it before thick fog intervened, leading to flight cancellations. The performance, therefore, featured prerecorded footage of Cheryl and Bobby walking around Jersey during the verses and the group lip-syncing from two locations: Cheryl and Bobby in St Helier, and Jay and Mike at the BBC Studios in London. The group also performed their new single 'Run For Your Life' in a similar fashion.

In 1985, a Spanish language version, 'Me Gusta Ser Sonrisa (I'd Like To Say I Love You)', was recorded by Mexican girl group trio Flans, who achieved widespread success in Mexico and Latin America. It was the opening track on their self-titled debut album, which sold over 100,000 copies. Some fans of the group have commented that the Flans cover surpasses the Bucks Fizz original, and whilst I respectfully disagree with that assertion, it makes me happy to see people appreciating a great pop song and hopefully discovering Bucks Fizz as a consequence.

'You Love, Love' (Andy Sells)

Released as a single in May 1989. Chart place: did not chart.

A highlight of the album is this beautiful ballad featuring a gorgeous lead vocal by Cheryl Baker. The thoughtful lyrics are addressed to someone who longs for the intoxicating rush of a new romance, who loves the feeling of being in love rather than an enduring relationship that matures and changes: 'Time moves on from storm to gentle breezes/The dizzy feeling leaves us/It's a dream you're dreaming of'.

The first half of the song consists of a solo vocal from Cheryl, piano and orchestra. Drums, bass and the other members of Bucks Fizz join in for the bridge section before it fades to leave piano, orchestra and Cheryl's vocal adorned by group harmonies at the song's conclusion. This song was beautifully captured in the group's *Rhythm On 2* TV special in 1983 (with a different mix, minus the strings, later included on *The Lost Masters 2*), and you would have to be astonishingly hard-hearted not to be moved by it. 'You Love, Love' was the only song written by Andy Sells that the group recorded. Andy began playing guitar and writing songs as a teenager, eventually working as a recording engineer, arranger and producer while continuing to write and perform. On his website, he comments, 'Along the way, I won a grand prize in the American Song Festival for 'You Love Love (More Than You Love Me)', which ended up on a top 20 album by the British pop group Bucks Fizz.' Ironically, this coincided with him opting out of the music business to start a family and pursue a different career path.

On *Are You Ready,* the two emotional ballads had been sung by Bobby and Mike, but on *Hand Cut,* lead vocals on the two ballads were by Jay and Cheryl. For the two preceding albums, the third single had been a slower track ('One Of Those Nights' and 'Now Those Days Are Gone', respectively), which perhaps pointed to 'You Love, Love' being a potential single. Mike Nolan told fans on Capital Radio in 1984 that 'You Love Love' was his favourite track on *Hand Cut,* but any single release should have been in 1983. By the time RCA released the track as a single, a little over six years later in May 1989, the moment had passed, and sadly, it became the only Bucks Fizz single that failed to chart. It was a shame that such an undeserved fate befell this beautiful song, but it was still nice to see Cheryl, Mike and Bobby interviewed on *TV AM* at the time of the single's release and perform an abridged version of the song live to piano accompaniment.

'Shot Me Through The Heart' (Andy Hill/Nichola Martin)
This track was released ahead of the album, appearing on the B-side of 'Run For Your Life'. It is a little lightweight compared to the tracks surrounding it, but for me, that is exactly the point, and it is an excellent bit of album sequencing. You've had the fabulous 'If You Can't Stand The Heat', followed by the soaring pop brilliance of 'I'd Like To Say I Love You', and then Cheryl's beautiful, fragile vocal on the gorgeous 'You Love Love' has just wrung your heart out (well, it certainly did mine!), so to have a song that doesn't demand so much of you is perfect. It is a moment of respite, a chance to gather the emotions before the final track.

Having said all of that, 'Shot Me Through The Heart' is a good song and sonically rather lovely. The gentle, electronic keyboards and soft harmonies of the introduction feel quite calming, but they are anchored by Andy Hill's bass and Graham Broad's thumping electronic percussion, which, besides the keyboards, provide the only instrumentation on the track. Mike and Bobby sing the lead in the verses, and their vocals have an almost phased effect before being joined by Cheryl, Jay and an uncredited Andy Hill for the layered harmonies of the chorus.

'Running Out Of Time' (Andy Hill/Ian Bairnson)

I bought *Hand Cut* on the way home from school on the day that it came out. By that time, I had already heard four of the tracks, the two singles, 'Shot Me Through The Heart' and 'I'd Like To Say I Love You'. Of the new songs that I heard that day, this was the one I initially gravitated towards, and it reminded me of all the reasons that I loved this group.

The first verse and chorus consist only of keyboards and percussion, with a solo vocal by Jay in the verses, before the whole group join in for the chorus. In the second verse, the group's harmonies begin to weave around Jay, with Cheryl and Jay's delightful vocals on the lines 'Then we all can fly/Out of the dark and into the light/Nobody would know' lifting the song skyward, before the whole group, drums, bass and guitars reinforce the song's tremendous hook line. Following a brief instrumental section, there is some intricate vocal interplay, with Bobby and Cheryl's voices prominent. The chorus returns once more, with Jay singing the refrain on her own this time, her lead vocal cushioned by layers of harmonies, electronic percussion and bass guitar. On her line 'I'm out of time…', Jay holds an impossibly long note, as the other members of Bucks Fizz sing the chorus and all the instruments return, with Graham Broad's drums and an additional keyboard melody providing the final flourishes.

Like so many of Bucks Fizz's finest moments, it is deceptively simple, whilst being beautifully, brilliantly and meticulously crafted pop music. A wonderful way to end a superb album.

Bonus Tracks

These four tracks can be found on *Hand Cut: The Definitive Edition* CD:

'Stepping Out' (Bucks Fizz)

Originally appearing on the B-side of 'If You Can't Stand The Heat', this was the second track written and produced by the group, and it is another excellent one. Mike sings the opening lines of the first two verses, with Cheryl and Jay supplying the answering phrases and the whole group joining in for the chorus. The guitar and bass parts are kept simple, and it is the drums and a synthesised rhythm that drive the track. I love the keyboard solo after the second chorus, which has a touch of Jean Michel-Jarre about it, and Cheryl's wordless vocals, which accompany this melody when it repeats for a second time, are wonderful. There is another cool moment towards the end of the track when the group introduce another vocal melody line in the chorus, and as the song fades, the vocals phase slightly. This track features reverb on the lead and backing vocals, which contrasts with the more intimate vocal sound employed on *Hand Cut* album tracks such as 'Shot Me Through The Heart' or 'Running Out Of Time'. Similarly, the instrumentation diverges from its parent album with more reverb on the drums and a simpler, keyboard-led sound. It might have sounded out of place on *Hand Cut* on account of its differing production style, but in terms of musical quality, this is a great pop song that more than warranted inclusion.

'If You Can't Stand The Heat (12" Version)' (Andy Hill/Ian Bairnson)
Exactly the same as the 7" version until 2.33, when it edits to a stripped-down version of the end section, minus the vocals. The first verse is repeated at 3.09, followed by an instrumental version of the chorus. The best part of the mix is from 4.21 onwards, with an instrumental version of the chorus with the guitar chords higher in the mix. When the group's vocals return, they do so with Graham Broad playing different drum patterns behind them.

'If You Can't Stand The Heat (Early Version)' (Andy Hill/Ian Bairnson)
The core of the song is here, but there are more ingredients yet to be added to the mix. Ian Bairnson's guitar riff in the verses is present, but it is absent in the introduction and much less prevalent throughout the song, as is Graham Broad's distinctive percussion and the brass parts. The vocals are slightly different, too, with more reverb on Mike and Bobby's vocals during the chorus and a 'dead ending' to the song, unlike the regular 7" and 12" versions, which fade out.

'Live Medley: Pinball Wizard/Hot Stuff/Do You Think I'm Sexy/Knock On Wood/Rocking All Over The World' (Pete Townshend/Pete Bellotte/Harold Faltermeyer/Keith Forsey/Rod Stewart/Carmine Appice/Duane Hitchings/Eddie Floyd/Steve Cropper/John Fogerty)
Flexipop was a monthly music magazine that ran for 33 issues from 1980 to 1983. It was brash and colourful, but its major selling point was that each issue featured a free flexi disc with an exclusive track. Previous issues had featured artists as diverse as The Jam, Adam and the Ants, Motorhead, Depeche Mode, Soft Cell, Altered Images, The Cure and Madness.

This track is an enjoyable studio version of a medley that Bucks Fizz were performing in their live concerts at the time, allowing each group member to share a lead vocal, beginning with 'Pinball Wizard' (Bobby), then 'Hot Stuff' (Jay), 'Do You Think I'm Sexy' (Mike) and 'Knock On Wood' (Cheryl) before ending with the whole group on 'Rocking All Over The World'. Although the

Bucks Fizz flexi was numbered *Flexipop* 024 – and was originally intended for the corresponding magazine – it actually came with issue 25 in December 1982 ('Discipline' by Marc Almond and Friends came with issue 24 and was numbered *Flexipop* 023A). The flexi was available in both light blue and green formats and was finally released on CD as a hidden bonus on the 2004 reissue of *Hand Cut*. It later appeared as a credited track on Cherry Pop's 2CD Definitive Edition in 2015; however, it differed slightly from the original *Flexipop* version as it featured audience cheering and applause added on at the start of the medley.

A further track appeared on *The Lost Masters*:

'I'd Like To Say I Love You (Alternate Take)' (Warren Harry)
A few subtle differences from the *Hand Cut* version, most notably on Bobby's vocal at 2.44, preceding the final chorus, which applies a phasing effect to his vocals, rendering it less effective. Another difference is the string section at the end, which fades earlier, shortening the song by 18 seconds.

These two additional tracks appeared on *The Lost Masters 2 – The Final Cut*:

'I'd Like To Say I Love You (Alternate Mix)' (Warren Harry)
This appears to be the mix used for the group's *Rhythm On Two* special, with the keyboards higher in the mix, omitting the strings, shortening the song by removing the second chorus after Jay's solo vocal and featuring a dead ending.

'You Love Love (TV Version)' (Andy Sells)
A mono mix of the track, minus the orchestral arrangement, as featured on the *Rhythm On Two* TV special. It would be nice to have a stereo version of this one day, as even without all the embellishments, it is a beautiful song with a gorgeous vocal from Cheryl.

Greatest Hits (1983)

Personnel:
Mike Nolan: lead vocals, backing vocals
Cheryl Baker: lead vocals, backing vocals
Bobby G: lead vocals, backing vocals
Jay Aston: lead vocals, backing vocals
Andy Hill: keyboards, bass, acoustic guitar, backing vocals
Graham Broad: drums and percussion
Ian Bairnson: guitar, bass
Richard Cottle: keyboards
Pete Wingfield: keyboards
John Read: bass
Chris Hunter: saxophone
Spike: trombone
Guy Barker: trumpet
Nichola Martin: backing vocals, keyboards
Alan Carvell: backing vocals
Nick Ingman: string arrangements
Recorded at Mayfair Studios, London; Morgan Studios, London; Marcus Studios, London; Utopia Studios, London; Power Plant, London; RG Jones Studio, Wimbledon; Comforts Place, Surrey, between March 1981 and October 1983
Producer: Andy Hill, Brian Tench
Engineers: John Hudson, Martin Webster, Brad Davis, Brian Tench, Bobby Parr
Photography: Brian Aris
UK release date: November 1983
Charts: UK: 25
Track Listing: 1. 'My Camera Never Lies', 2. 'London Town', 3. 'Piece Of The Action', 4. 'Now Those Days Are Gone', 5. 'Making Your Mind Up', 6. 'When We Were Young', 7. 'Land Of Make Believe', 8. 'One Of Those Nights', 9. 'Oh Suzanne', 10. 'If You Can't Stand The Heat', 11. 'Run For Your Life', 12. 'Rules Of The Game'
Please note, Greatest Hits contained no credits except the songwriters, production and photography. These credits have been compiled using known information about the constituent tracks from the first three albums

Although ostensibly a compilation album, *Greatest Hits* was a strange and pivotal moment in the trajectory of Bucks Fizz. The group's three studio albums had followed a pattern; a lead single well in advance of the album, ('Making Your Mind Up', 'The Land Of Make Believe', 'If You Can't Stand The Heat'), a second single closer to the release date, ('Piece Of The Action', 'My Camera Never Lies', 'Run For Your Life') and a third single, usually a ballad, taken from it ('One Of Those Nights', 'Now Those Days Are Gone'). *Hand Cut* had deviated from this last part as 'When We Were Young' had been issued as a standalone single instead, but this had paid off, earning the group another UK top ten hit in the summer of 1983.

In their July 1983 fan club newsletter, Bucks Fizz highlighted their preparations for two weeks of shows at Cornwall Coliseum, St Austell, from 1 to 13 August 1983. They announced that they were working on a new album with a proposed Christmas release date and were performing seven shows over five days (including two matinees) at the Apollo Theatre, Victoria, London, from 27 to 31 December 1983. The group's message also stated, 'Our next single will be released around 9 September and is called 'Invisible'. September came, but instead of 'Invisible', the single was 'London Town', which reached number 34 in the UK charts. Addressing this change in the November 1983 newsletter, the group's fan club secretary, Gay Purle, wrote:

> I mentioned in the last newsletter that the next single would be 'Invisible' and then, of course, it was 'London Town'. This confused lots of you, but this was the information I was given at that time, which obviously changed. Before you all ask, 'Invisible' will not be released as a single. I also told you that a brand new album would be released in November; this, too, has changed, and that album will not be released until spring 1984. However, in November, the Bucks Fizz *Greatest Hits* album will be released due to popular demand.

In November, 'Rules Of The Game' became the group's third single in six months, peaking at a disappointing number 57, with Jay later telling *Look In,* 'It didn't get played. It came out too soon after 'London Town', and it got a bit lost among all the Christmas stuff.' *Greatest Hits* followed shortly afterwards and featured another new track, 'Oh Suzanne', a fascinating collision of songwriting styles between Andy Hill and Warren Bacall, who had written 'When We Were Young' and 'Rules Of The Game'. A Bucks Fizz compilation album had been nowhere in sight at the time 'London Town' was released, and with the group recording tracks for a new album, *Greatest Hits* seemed to represent a change of plan, or perhaps an opportunity that presented itself. A third of this album was newer material recorded since *Hand Cut,* and at the time, it seemed to be a way of taking stock, charting the evolution of Bucks Fizz over the previous two and a half years, whilst introducing the group's changing sound and image by combining it with familiar hit songs. In hindsight, though, the decision not to release 'Invisible' or 'Oh Suzanne' as singles, both tracks which originally featured Jay on lead vocals, was also a change of plan. Arguably, building a fourth studio album around them, with 'London Town' and 'Rules Of The Game' as album tracks, might have proved a commercially stronger option. A compilation of the group's first nine singles, possibly including a new song and selected album tracks in the manner of ABBA's *Greatest Hits Vol. 2,* would still have made for a worthy *Greatest Hits* release that Christmas.

The sleeve to 'Rules Of The Game' and *Greatest Hits* featured a *Let It Be*-style cover of four individual headshots of the group members, taken by photographer Brian Aris, framed against a black background. Another photo session of the group from late 1983 depicts them as explorers, making their way through a tropical jungle, and includes one particularly striking image of three of the group looking away and only Cheryl looking directly at the camera. Oddly, it was scenes from this photo shoot that were featured in the TV commercial for *Greatest Hits,* so why this was done and then not used for the album cover itself is a bit of a mystery. Later copies of the album featured a slightly amended sleeve with a competition to win a day in Paris with Bucks Fizz (for ages 6-17) or a Mini Sprite for ages 18 and over. In 1984, *Greatest Hits* became one of the earliest releases by RCA on the newly emerging compact disc format, and, until the release of *Writing On The Wall* in 1986, it was the only Bucks Fizz album available in this format. It was reissued in 1986, but not since then, which means that the wealth of material released at this time – three singles, an exclusive track, two extended versions, two B-sides, a 12" bonus track, plus the intended 12" mix of 'Rules Of The Game' and original versions of 'Oh Suzanne' – is often grouped together with *Hand Cut,* even though the tracks were recorded after it.

Writing in *Number One,* Paul Bursche said, 'They're all here, and all displaying that sameness and forced jollity which has made Bucks Fizz what they are today – a bubbly cocktail guaranteed not to disturb stomach or stir brain.' Betty Page in *Record Mirror* also criticised the similarity of the songs, 'which only sounds good in three-minute bursts on the radio' and described 'Now Those Days Are Gone' as 'the only truly different thing they've ever done.'

Personally, I loved this era of Bucks Fizz; their image was becoming more provocative, inventive, outlandish and unpredictable – all fuelled by Jay Aston's fashion flair and imagination. As a fan, this was exciting as I had no idea what image the group would come up with next, but in a wider sense, it also opened me up to the idea that fashion could be creative and fun and not just something bought from a store. There were also changes musically, with two of the three post *Hand Cut* singles being written by Warren Bacall, a new writer to the group, which led Bucks Fizz down a musically heavier and lyrically much darker path. 'When We Were Young' is a song about a woman observing the ageing process in herself and mourning the loss of love and her youthful beauty. 'Rules Of The Game' concerns someone who is seduced by fame and adulation and neglects a relationship as a consequence. It contains the idea that love is a ballet, or a game, a delicate balancing act between the demands of the ego and the deeper needs of the heart. These were more mature themes for a young audience that was growing up with the group, and the way Bucks Fizz approached these songs changed to suit the material. Both Jay (on 'When We Were Young') and Cheryl (on 'Rules Of The Game' and 'Oh Suzanne') adopted a dramatic, affected vocal that was closer in style to Hazel O'Connor than the light, bright tones of *Are You Ready* only 18 months earlier. In August 1983, Jay was quoted in *Sunday* magazine as saying, 'Our image is changing drastically, and from now on, we're going to become a much harder, stronger type of rock band. We're now leagues away from the type of group we were when we won the contest, but now we want to make as big a jump again.' As a card-carrying rock fan whose other favourite 1983 albums besides *Hand Cut* included records by Yes, Electric Light Orchestra, Def Leppard, Genesis and Asia, the fact that Bucks Fizz were heading in a more rock-oriented direction suited me just fine. In the programme notes for their Christmas shows at the London Apollo, the group wrote:

> Since our last tour of England in March and April, it seems as though we have not stopped working and travelling. We have travelled all over Europe this summer, doing television appearances and interviews for the press, and in between, we flew to South America and Bahrain to do two concerts. We have also been recording new material, some of it written by Bobby, for our next album, which comes out in May 1984.

As it turned out, however, the next album would take a little longer than that.

'When We Were Young' (Warren Bacall)
Released as a single in June 1983. Chart place: UK: 10
'When We Were Young' was unexpected; a startling change of direction with a musically heavier and lyrically much darker song about a woman growing older, losing her looks and becoming depressed by it. 'The song is totally different to anything we've ever done before', Cheryl told *Look In* magazine at the time, whilst in an interview with *Record Mirror* in May 1983, ahead of the single's release, Jay Aston said:

> It's a very different kind of song. I've racked my brains trying to label it, and I can't. It's much harder and heavier, and I'm pleased about that. It's time for a new direction for Bucks Fizz. You've got to move with the times. I think that's one of the things that has kept Bucks Fizz alive, the fact that we do take a fresh look at things and keep on the move. We'll probably lose a lot of our old fans with this single, but I hope we'll interest lots of new people, too.

Later in the same article, writer Daniela Soave remarked, 'A sneak preview of the single soon proves that you'd never for a minute connect it with Bucks Fizz if you weren't told.' This proved to be correct when the track was played on the Radio One new releases programme *Roundtable* on Friday 27 May. The panel were not told in advance who the artist was, and none of them discerned that the track was by Bucks Fizz.

The song was written by Warren Bacall, who, under the name Warren Harry, had written 'I'd Like To Say I Love You' on *Hand Cut*. This was a much darker song, though, with a bleakness and melancholy at its core, and the lyrics of the second verse stating, 'Youth it passes while age is collected/Disappear from behind blue eyes without trace', whilst the chorus repeats an almost nihilistic refrain of 'Love has gone, tears are here, nothing left'. Musically, it inhabits a heavier soundscape than anything on *Hand Cut,* released only three months previously. It was the first single on which production credits were shared by Andy Hill and Brian Tench, and the first single to feature solo lead vocals by Jay, who adopted a notably different, affected voice on this track, as she later told the *Vinyl Vibes* podcast:

> The original demo ... was a very weird, affected voice. There had been a track called 'Breaking Glass' (by Hazel O'Connor) which had been a big success ... and the vocal on that was quite affected. Well, I'm quite good at changing my voice. I can mimic things. I can be a character. Andy (Hill) wanted this affected vocal. Cheryl hated it; she still takes the mickey out of me today for singing it.

Jay's vocal was unlike anything Fizz fans had heard from her before, but she absolutely owns this song, delivering a powerful and dramatic performance with the group supporting her on the chorus and the latter part of the second verse. There is a clever arrangement towards the end of the song when, at 2.50, everything stops apart from the keyboards and Cheryl and Jay's vocals, making it much more impactful when all the instrumentation comes crashing in at once. From 3.17, Andy Hill adds additional backing vocals, building up a wall of sound, before Bobby adds the final touch, singing the title of the song repeatedly over the chorus of voices. It was a wonderful but very different single. It took some getting used to. However, it deservedly gave Bucks Fizz another top ten hit in the summer of 1983.

The single was released on 3 June 1983 in both 7" and 12" formats. The B-side was 'Where The Ending Starts', also featuring Jay on lead vocal. The 12" single featured an 'Extended Club Mix' of the track and a very strong bonus track entitled 'When The Love Has Gone'. There were 7" and 12" picture discs to collect, each featuring different pictures from the same photo shoot and a transparent green vinyl 7" single, released only in Germany (RCA Victor PB 68065).

The reviews, as was often the case, were not positive. *Record Mirror* stated, 'The puppets come out of the box again, all wiggling thighs and plastic smiles. Deadly attempt to put some fresh life into the act with a Bonnie Tyler-esque epic.' Mark Cooper, writing in *Number One,* described it as 'Their biggest and brassiest yet', though his comment that Bucks Fizz 'have the entire cast of *War And Peace* playing drums, and that's only in the background' made me smile.

Initial TV performances on *Razzmatazz* on 7 June 1983 (Episode 10) and *Cheggers Plays Pop* on 8 June 1983 (Episode 55) were atypical for the group, with Jay as the focal point and Cheryl sitting at the rear of the stage with

Bobby to her left and Mike on her right. This staging evolved for subsequent TV appearances, including their first *Top Of The Pops* appearance on 30 June 1983 (Episode 1005), which featured Cheryl sat astride a chair at the front of the stage, unveiling a striking, new slicked back hairstyle with a kiss curl that would feature on the picture sleeves of the next two singles and on the cover of the *Greatest Hits* album itself, with the rest of the group standing and Jay to her left. This staging was repeated for numerous European TV appearances and the group's second performance of the song on the 1983 Christmas Day edition of *Top Of The Pops* (Episode 1031).

'When We Were Young' was the highest new entry on the UK chart at number 23 on Tuesday 14 June 1983, which led to the promotional video being shown on *Top Of The Pops* the following Thursday (Episode 1003). This video was filmed in Germany and was later described by Jay as 'the cheapest video we ever did'. Having performed in Germany, the group had stayed at the home of Michael 'Mike' Leckebusch, producer and director of *Beat Club, Extratour* and *Muzik Laden*. Michael also directed music videos and had a video editing suite in his basement, so the video for 'When We Were Young' was filmed at his home. The latter half of the video features the group filmed against a brightly coloured chroma key background and superimposed over images of electricity pylons. Leckebusch liked the video, had produced it and featured it regularly on his show, which helped the song to become a hit in mainland Europe. In addition to being a top ten hit in the UK and Ireland, the song was a minor hit in Germany and a top 20 hit in the Netherlands, Belgium and Austria. The group went on to perform the song at the Montreux Golden Rose Pop Festival in May 1984.

'London Town' (Andy Hill)

Released as a single in September 1983. Chart place: UK: 34

Released as an 11th-hour replacement for 'Invisible' came the anxious, juddering 'London Town'. Bobby takes lead vocal on the track but made clear his dislike of the track, telling *Number One* magazine in 1984, 'My voice was treated, and I sound like a munchkin.' There are also distorted, sped-up, unintelligible vocals during the song's keyboard introduction, which belong to drummer Graham Broad. Personally, I think Andy Hill's production is top drawer, and the effects on Bobby's voice during the verses suit the song and the lyric, as if framing it like a character in a story against the more natural voices surrounding it. There are some lovely, effective harmonies in unexpected places, including the lead-up to Ian Bairnson's superb guitar solo (played on a Gibson 335), which is reminiscent of his equally glorious guitar solo at the end of Pilot's 'Penny In My Pocket'.

'London Town' is unusual subject matter for a pop single, a newcomer in the city, experiencing alienation and paranoia: 'Hostile faces all around/I really wish I'd stayed home/More punches knock me down/Looks like I'm all alone'. The second verse adds a sense of depersonalisation as it states: 'Oh please don't get me wrong I'm fine/I'm really, really gonna like it/You beat me, I don't mind/I'm a social misfit', as if the person is emotionally detaching themselves from these brutal experiences. And yet, for all that, London Town is where they want and intend to be: 'I am here to stay/And nobody will make me go away'.

Reaction to the song was a little muted, with Lenny Henry noting in *Smash Hits* 'I like some of their songs, but this one's a bit overproduced (understatement!) and lacks melody. Good drum pattern.' This feeling was reflected in the disappointing UK chart placing as the single peaked at number 34, the lowest charting single for the group up to that point, which broke a run of nine consecutive top 20 hits. The single fared better in other European territories, though, most notably Ireland, Austria and, in particular, Poland, where it was a top ten hit.

The promotional video, partially filmed at the former Holloway Sanatorium near Virginia Water, features Bobby as a besuited office worker, Jay creating a number of fierce and striking looks, and the group at a London tube station or bathed in the neon glow of televisions as a number of dancers move around them, the latter being an unusual feature for a Bucks Fizz video. Look out, too, for a couple of subtle humorous touches, such as the policeman playing air guitar to Ian Bairnson's solo or the newspaper placard as Bobby enters his place of work, which reads, 'BF Says: Wish we'd stayed home'. Pictures taken on the set of the video by *Smash Hits* in October 1983 show Jay with her elder brother, Lance Aston, who was cast as an extra in the video. The group appeared on *Top Of The Pops* on 13 October 1983 (Episode 1020), but there were several other TV appearances to promote the single, including *The Late, Late Breakfast Show, Harty, Pebble Mill At One* and *Musik Laden*.

The single was released in a picture sleeve (RCA 363) and as a 7" picture disc (RCAP 363) with a new track, 'Identity', on the B-side. The 12" single (RCAT 363) featured an extended version of the A-side and added 'Love Dies Hard' from the *Are You Ready* album. Worth looking out for is the German 7" release of the single (RCA Victor PB 68109) and the corresponding 12" (RCA Victor PC 68110), which feature a different sleeve to the UK issue.

'Rules Of The Game' (Warren Bacall)

Released as a single in November 1983. Chart place: UK: 57

'The rules seem to be that you release a single that sounds like (the) last one played faster and backwards', said Robin Smith in *Record Mirror*. Dave Rimmer in *Smash Hits* described the track as an 'Unremarkable and painless piece of Euro-Disco singalong with clattery noises and warbly vocals. Not as messy as their last one but every bit as boring.' It would be hard for me to overstate just how completely I disagree with these assessments.

In some ways, releasing 'Rules Of The Game' as a single made commercial sense: 'London Town' had been the group's lowest charting single so far, so why not return to the person who had written the group's most recent top ten hit? In other ways, it was a bold decision, to put it mildly. This was a sound and a look some distance removed from the Bucks Fizz of even a year ago, and to release this darkly dramatic song with its ferocious production as a single right in the run-up to Christmas made zero concessions to the festive season. The vocals, described as 'warbly' in the *Smash Hits* review, included an affected lead vocal from Cheryl, and 'Rules Of The Game' was the first time that this had been heard on record. As a fan, I loved this and I wondered where on earth Cheryl had found that voice from, but for the casual listener, 'Rules Of The Game' may not have been what they expected from or even recognised as Bucks Fizz. As for me, I bought 'Rules Of The Game' (without hearing it first) in November 1983, and I loved it immediately. It was confirmation that from one single to the next, I had no idea where Bucks Fizz might go with their image or their music, and I was thrilled by that. I thought it was an exciting single then, and I still do.

Bucks Fizz appeared on TV to promote the single throughout December and into the new year, including *Sunday Sunday* on 4 December 1983, *Razzmatazz* on 13 December 1983 (Episode 64), *Little And Large Show* on 17 December 1983, *Cheggers Plays Pop* on 30 December 1983 (Episode 56), and the *1983 Team Disco Championships,* introduced by Peter Powell, which aired on 4 January 1984. It transpired later that only Cheryl, Mike and Bobby featured on 'Rules Of The Game', as Cheryl shared on the bonus disc of *The Bucks Fizz Story* DVD, 'The words are, 'Love is the ballet where the dancer falls', and, because she didn't sing on the track, she (Jay) sung what she thought the words were: 'Love is the valley where the dancer falls'.' This was apparent on certain TV appearances, but I thought little of it at the time. I just enjoyed seeing the group performing their excellent new single and unveiling a series of striking looks on each occasion. There was a promotional video, too, featuring the group as moderators in a game involving martial arts, and although this has had an official release, it is not easy to track down, so a visit to YouTube is your best option.

Despite the TV appearances, the song performed relatively poorly, becoming the first Bucks Fizz single to miss the top 40, peaking at number 57 in the UK, although it remained in the top 75 for six weeks. Seven-inch copies came in a picture sleeve, replicating the image on the *Greatest Hits* album cover, backed by a new song, 'When We Were At War'. A second 7" featured a different sleeve and was a gatefold Christmas edition. A 12" single with an extended mix was prepared but appears not to have progressed beyond acetate copies.

'Oh Suzanne' (Andy Hill/Warren Bacall)

All the indications are that 'Oh Suzanne', initially with Jay on lead vocals, was being lined up as the group's 11th single, and rightly so, as it is a perfect fusion of Andy Hill's melodic sensibilities and Warren Bacall's dark, melodramatic style. This version features Cheryl on lead vocals and was included as an

Above: An early promotional photograph of Bucks Fizz at the time of 'Making Your Mind Up'. Left to right: Cheryl Baker, Bobby G, Jay Aston and Mike Nolan.

Below: The group promoting their compilation album *The Story So Far* (1988). Left to right: Mike Nolan, Cheryl Baker, Bobby G and Shelley Preston. The group toured in support of the album during April and May 1989. (*Alamy*)

Left: *Bucks Fizz* (1981). The group's debut album, featuring 'One Of Those Nights', 'Piece Of The Action' and 'Making Your Mind Up'. The khaki look on the cover came from Nichola Martin. (*RCA*)

Right: Surprisingly, 'Making Your Mind Up' didn't have a 7" picture sleeve in the UK. Fortunately, there were many lovely ones from around the world, including this one from Japan. (*RCA*)

Left: The group's sound and image were already changing with the release of their second single, 'Piece Of The Action', in 1981. (*RCA*)

Right: The group's biggest commercial and critical success. *Are You Ready* gave the group two number one singles in the UK with 'My Camera Never Lies' and 'The Land Of Make Believe'. (*RCA*)

Left: 'The Land Of Make Believe' (1981) became the group's biggest-selling single in the UK and their second number one. Limited edition copies featured this cardboard outer sleeve and a poster. (*RCA*)

Right: *Bucks Fizz* (1982) was the first album by the group released in North America. It was a compilation featuring eight of the tracks from *Are You Ready* and two from the group's first album. (*RCA*)

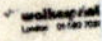

Above: Bucks Fizz performing 'Making Your Mind Up' at the *Eurovision Song Contest* in Dublin on 4 April 1981. They became the fourth act from the United Kingdom to win the contest, and their iconic routine is still remembered over four decades later.

Left: A signed photograph of Bucks Fizz from their Fan Club in 1982.

Right: Following the release of *Are You Ready,* the group embarked on a UK tour throughout July and August. This is the cover of the tour programme.

Left: A Bucks Fizz Fan Club embroidered patch from 1982.

Left: The spectacular *Hand Cut* (1983) produced two more top 20 hits for Bucks Fizz with 'If You Can't Stand The Heat' and 'Run For Your Life'. (*RCA*)

Right: 'Run For Your Life' (1983) was the group's eighth consecutive top 20 hit in the UK. The 7" picture sleeve saw the group looking incredibly glamorous whilst fleeing from an erupting volcano! (*RCA*)

Left: *Greatest Hits* (1983) brought together the group's first 11 singles and the exclusive track 'Oh Suzanne'. In 1984, it became one of the first releases by RCA on the newly emerging compact disc format. (*RCA*)

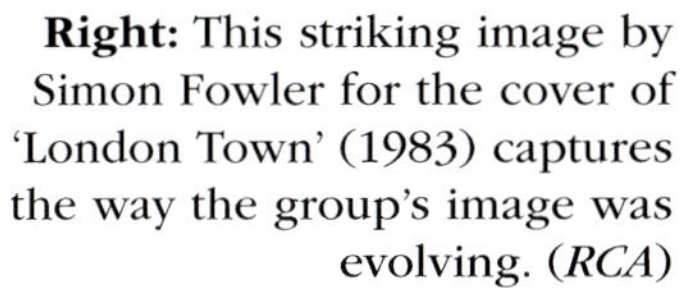

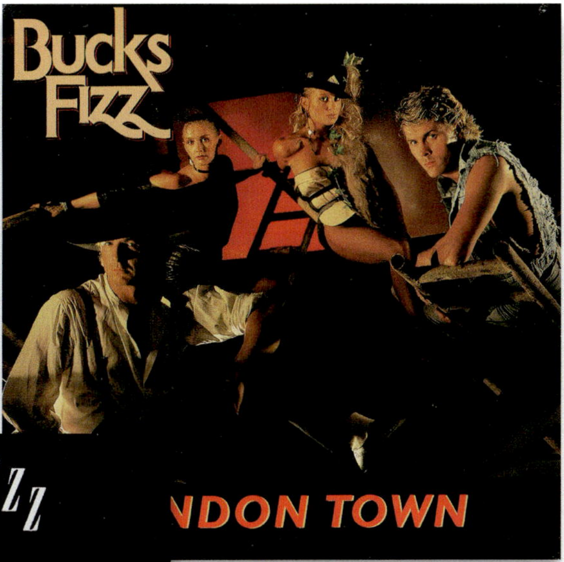

Right: This striking image by Simon Fowler for the cover of 'London Town' (1983) captures the way the group's image was evolving. (*RCA*)

Left: *I Hear Talk* (1984) was a darker and much more sombre affair, as reflected in this moody shot of the group taken at Camber Sands that graced the album cover. (*RCA*)

Right: The only Bucks Fizz album to feature Shelley Preston, *Writing On The Wall* (1986) was an amalgamation of tracks recorded in 1985 for RCA and others recorded for the group's new label, Polydor. (*Polydor*)

Left: A promotional poster for *Hand Cut*. The album was released in March 1983, and the group set off on a Nationwide tour in the same month.

ODEON THEATRE, Birmingham

Barry Dickins & Rod Macsween for I.T.B. in Association with Razzamatazz presents—

BUCKS FIZZ in Concert

Tuesday, 22nd March 1983

Evening 7.30

CENTRE STALLS

£5.00

Z 23

NO TICKET EXCHANGED NOR MONEY REFUNDED
THIS PORTION TO BE RETAINED (P.T.O.)

A. B. Cooper (Printers) Ltd. Manchester

Right: My first Bucks Fizz concert: Birmingham Odeon, 22 March 1983. I spent a lot of pocket money at the merchandise stall.

Right: The cover of the group's 1984 tour programme. The tour began in Blackpool on 3 May and ended in Cardiff on 19 June.

BUCKS FIZZ 1984

BUCKS FIZZ

I hear talk

THEIR NEW SINGLE
ON 7" & 12" Extended version
OUT NEXT WEEK

APPEARING ON TELEVISION
'HOGMANAY' New Year's Eve BBC 1
'PEBBLE MILL AT 1·00' 4th Jan. BBC 1
'RAZZMATAZZ' 9th Jan. ITV

ON TOUR – DECEMBER
19th CARDIFF – St David's Hall
20th BIRMINGHAM – Odeon
21st WEMBLEY Conference Centre
23rd CROYDON Fairfield Halls

CANCELLED

RCA

Left: A magazine cutting following the group's coach crash in Newcastle in December 1984.

Left: All change with Shelley Preston on the cover of 'Magical' (1985). Shelley joined Bucks Fizz at the start of July and had just six weeks to prepare for a nationwide tour. (*RCA*)

Right: The epic 'New Beginning' (1986) was the first single with Shelley and restored Bucks Fizz to the top ten. Limited edition copies came with a poster sleeve. (*Polydor*)

Left: 'Keep Each Other Warm' (1986) was the final single released from *Writing On The Wall*. A limited-edition double pack 7" was released ahead of the album, enabling fans to listen to excerpts of all ten tracks. (*Polydor*)

Right: In 1988, Stylus Records licensed 18 tracks from RCA and Polydor for *The Story So Far* (1988). It included the group's most recent single, 'Heart Of Stone'. (*Stylus*)

Left: Not one of their biggest hits, but one of their best songs. 'Heart Of Stone' (1988) would later be covered by Cher, who made it the title track of her album. (*RCA*)

Right: A copy of *Smoke And Mirrors* (2020), signed by Cheryl, Mike and Jay of The Fizz. (*MPG*)

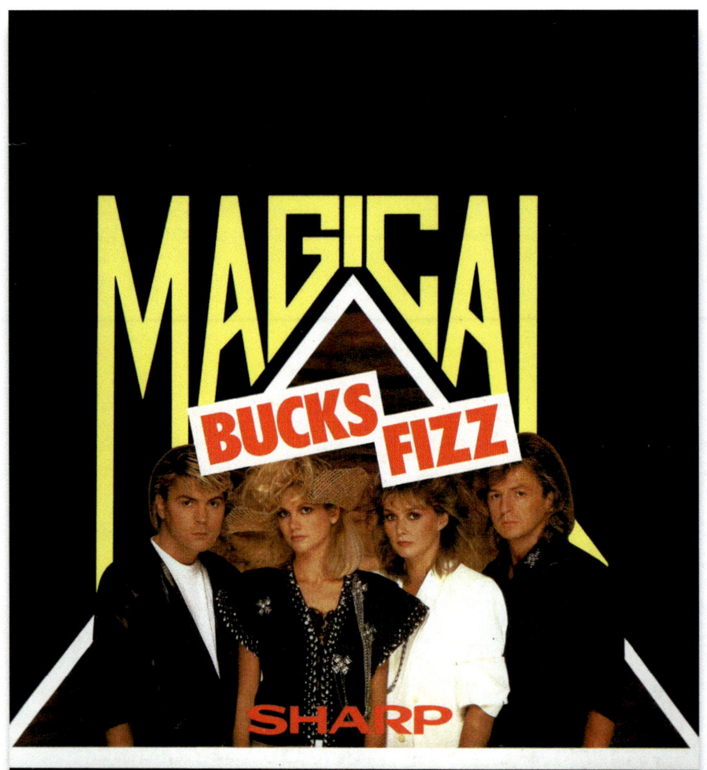

Left: The cover of the *Magical Tour* programme from 1985. It was Shelley Preston's first tour with the group, and it ran from 17 August 1985 to 5 October 1985.

Blackpool Winter Gardens and Opera House

J 23

OPERA HOUSE, BLACKPOOL

SHARP
presents BUCKS FIZZ
1st House 6-0

STALLS

SAT.
OCT.
5th

THIS PORTION TO BE RETAINED
VAT No.: 341 1854 76

1985

Examine Tickets before leaving Box Office. Mistakes cannot be rectified afterwards. No ticket exchanged or money refunded

Right: A ticket for the last day of the *Magical Tour* at Blackpool Winter Gardens in October 1985.

Above: A photo shoot from July 1985, following the announcement of Shelley Preston as the new member of the group. (*Alamy*)

Left: In 1984, Bucks Fizz embarked on a massive UK tour with a suitably Orwellian theme. The limited-edition *Talking In Your Sleep* EP captured the group at the Glasgow Apollo. (*RCA*)

Right: 'You And Your Heart So Blue' (1985) coincided with Jay leaving Bucks Fizz, but she still featured on the cover of the limited-edition EP, which featured cover versions of 'Censored' and 'One Touch (Don't Mean Devotion)'. (*RCA*)

Left: In 1982, Bucks Fizz recorded a Spanish-language album, *El Mundo De Ilusion,* which was released in Argentina, Bolivia and Chile. (*RCA*)

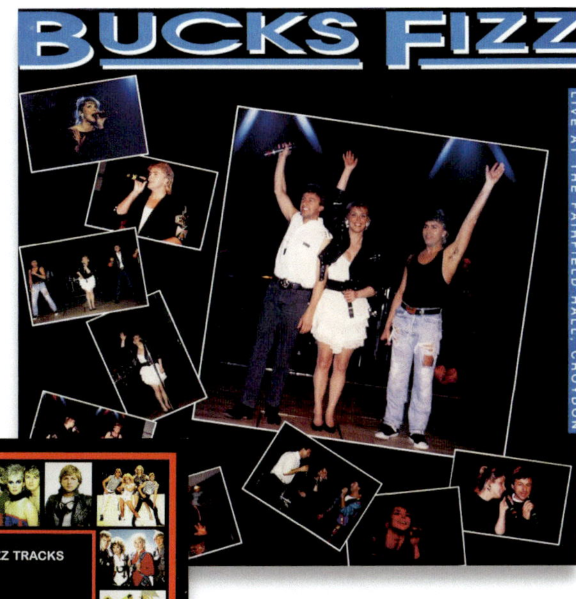

Right: By 1991, Bucks Fizz were a trio of Bobby, Cheryl and Mike for *Live At The Fairfield Hall, Croydon*. It was the group's only live album and their only release on Jet Records. (*Jet Records*)

Left: The 2CD set *The Lost Masters* (2006) was an absolute treasure trove of previously unreleased extended mixes, alternate versions, demos and previously unheard solo and group material. (*Sony/BMG*)

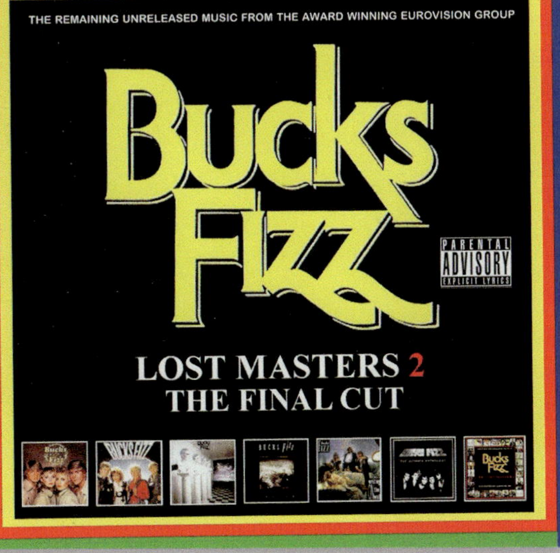

Right: *Lost Masters 2 – The Final Cut* (2008) was another bumper helping of demos, alternate versions, unreleased material and newly created remixes. (*Sony/BMG*)

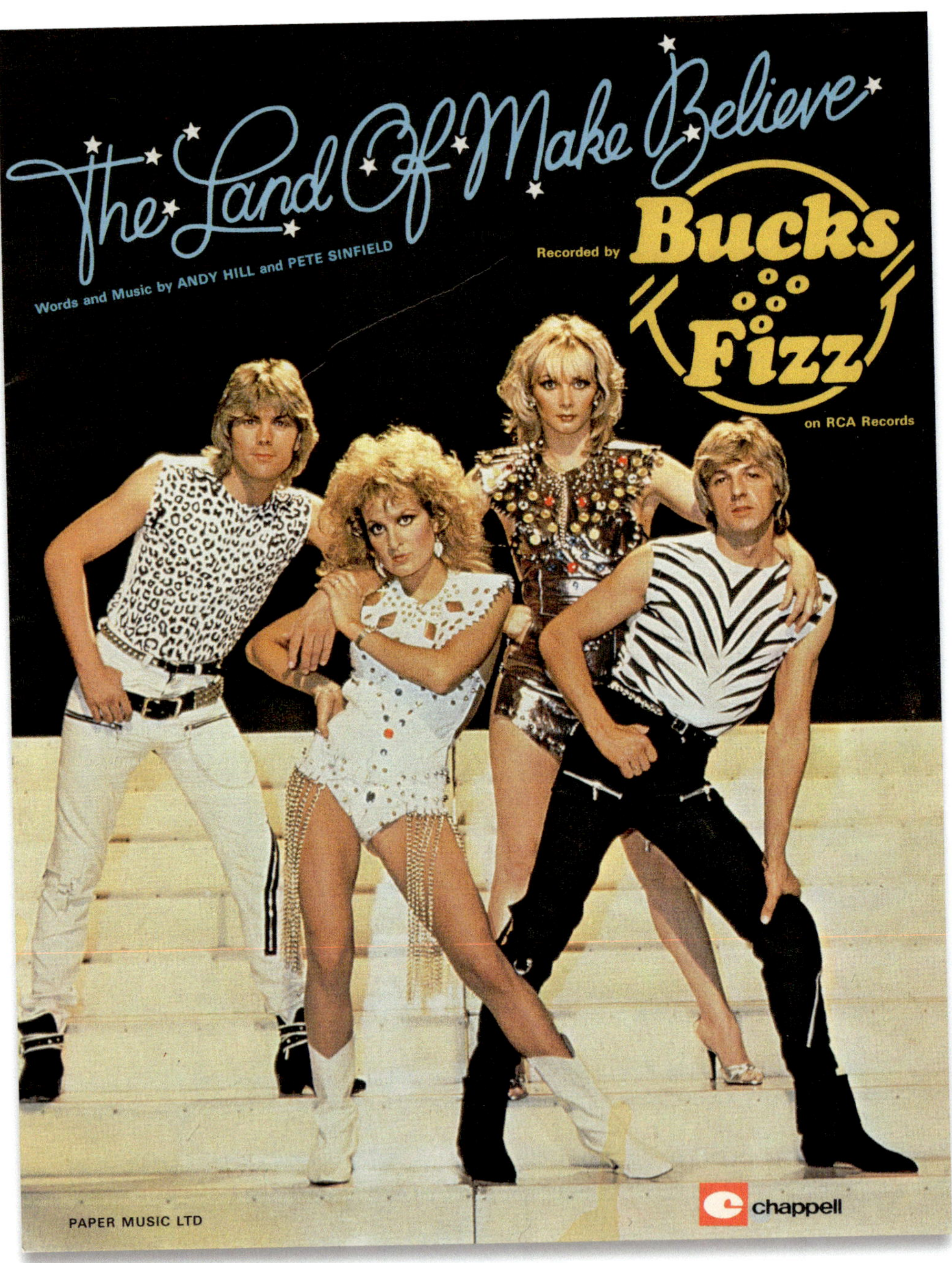

Above: The sheet music to 'The Land Of Make Believe', highlighting the unique look Jay created for the group in the video.

exclusive, previously unreleased track on *Greatest Hits*. It was an additional incentive for Fizz fans to buy the album, but it was also a waste of a tremendous single-worthy track.

'Oh Suzanne' has long been one of my favourite Bucks Fizz songs, with its relentless synthesised bass, driving electric guitar riff, a superb brass arrangement that emphasises the guitar riff but adds its own melodic flourishes, punchy backing vocals and a wonderfully dramatic, affected vocal from Cheryl. It also contains one of my favourite lyrics in a pop song, 'So when you hear her calling in the dead of night, don't answer/'Cos a broken heart and a broken mind spells danger'. It would have made a great single, and notably, it was retained in the group's setlist throughout their 1984 and 1985 tours as a solo number for Cheryl.

The track later appeared as the B-side to 'Magical' in 1985, and the original version with Jay on vocals was rescued and restored in 7" and 12" form on *The Lost Masters* in 2006. Both versions can more readily be found now among the 'post *Hand Cut'* material on disc two of *Hand Cut: The Definitive Edition*.

Bonus Tracks

The following seven tracks were included on *Hand Cut: The Definitive Edition* CD:

'When The Love Has Gone' (Andy Hill/Nichola Martin)

This song originally appeared as a bonus track on the 'When We Were Young' 12" single. It takes the group's sound on *Hand Cut* and gives it a dance-oriented makeover, with bright keyboards and electric rhythm guitar lending the opening a Shalamar-esque feel, which is never a bad thing. It is gloriously and unmistakably Bucks Fizz, though, with Bobby on lead, Mike providing vocals on the bridge section and the group adding some great harmonies on the chorus. It would have sounded out of place on the group's next album, *I Hear Talk,* but surrounded by other songs from 1983, such as 'When We Were Young', 'Oh Suzanne', 'London Town' and 'Invisible', it could potentially have been an album track. It was certainly far too good to remain just a bonus track on a 12" single.

'When We Were Young (Extended Club Mix)' (Warren Bacall)

The original 12" single mix, which features an extended instrumental section beginning at 2.23. The instrumentation is initially sparse when the group's vocals return, and the end section of the song is slightly longer, with the guitars prominent. There is also an additional vocal line from Bobby that was cut from the 7" version.

'Identity' (Bucks Fizz)

Produced by Bobby G, this track was originally the B-side to 'London Town'. It is quite a short song (2.37) and feels a little insubstantial compared to the group's previous self-penned B-sides. There are elements of the song that I like, though, most notably Mike's lead vocal on the verses, Jay's solo vocal after the second chorus and a chorus that is stronger melodically than the verses.

'London Town (Extended Club Mix)' (Andy Hill)

Although I think 'Invisible' would have been a better single choice, I have a lot of love for 'London Town'; the song, the fashion, the performances, the promotional video and, in particular, this fantastic extended version that featured on the 12" single. It does not so much remix the track as redesign it. It dispenses with the introduction used on the 7" single and begins with an instrumental version of the chorus, initially consisting of just some of the keyboard parts and the drums. This chorus is repeated five times with further keyboards, instrumentation and finally the group's vocals gradually being added before it jumps to the guitar refrain preceding the first verse.

On the 7" version, following the lines 'Is this the right place for the rat race that I play', the chorus is repeated five times to fade out, with Mike Nolan's processed vocals coming in for the third chorus. This section appears for the first time in this mix at 3.11, but with some of the keyboard parts removed from the start of the third chorus, along with Mike's vocal after his first 'I am in love with London Town' line. Following this, all of the instrumentation is removed except for the drums and the group's vocals consist of the words 'In London Town' with a repeat echo effect applied. At 4.25, this mix jumps to the instrumental section of 'London Town', but it is almost unrecognisable as it consists of just drums, sparse keyboards and female vocals repeating the word 'Town' (twice), again with a repeat echo effect. This 'Extended Club Mix' then repeats the song's instrumental section twice, the first without Ian Bairnson's excellent guitar solo, followed by a second one that includes it. By shuffling sections of 'London Town' around and stripping away parts of it, this version reveals hidden elements of the song that perhaps went unnoticed on the single, creating an atmosphere and a mix that is far superior to its 7" counterpart. I practically wore out my copy of this as a teenager, and it is my personal favourite of all the Bucks Fizz extended mixes.

'When We Were At War' (Bucks Fizz)

In his piece for *The Guardian,* Bob Stanley referred to Andy Hill's 'magpie tendencies', which included 'the glacial drama of Foreigner's 'Waiting For A Girl Like You' applied to 'When We Were at War'.' However, in this instance, the credit belongs to Bucks Fizz, who wrote the song, and to Bobby G, who produced it. It originally appeared as the B-side to 'Rules Of The Game' and its serene reflection on a relationship gone awry contrasts with its more frenetic A-side. With Bobby on lead vocals, Cheryl prominent on backing vocals and clocking in just short of six minutes, it is not one of the group's better-known songs. It is lovely though and deserved to have a place on the next album.

'Rules Of The Game (12" Version)' (Warren Bacall)
This extended mix was created in 1983. A release was planned for a 12" single, and it was even allocated a catalogue number (RCA RCAT380), but it seems never to have materialised. In all my years of collecting Bucks Fizz, I have never seen a copy, nor do I know of anyone who has, and the only proof of its existence that I am aware of is a picture of the label on an acetate copy. The mix itself remained in the vault for 17 years, finally emerging as a bonus track on the first CD edition of *Are You Ready* in 2000.

'Oh Suzanne (Jay Aston Version)' (Andy Hill/Warren Bacall)
A previously unreleased version of the track, featuring Jay on lead vocals rather than Cheryl, that first appeared on *The Lost Masters* in 2006. Confusingly, on *The Lost Masters,* this was titled as the '7" Unreleased Version', but on streaming sites, the mix with Cheryl's lead is sometimes billed as the 7" version, although neither track was actually a single! Two great versions of a fabulous track – pick your favourite.

'Oh Suzanne (Extended Version)' (Andy Hill/Warren Bacall)
This extended version featuring Jay on lead vocals was created in 1983 but remained unreleased until 2006. It begins with the drum break that occurred at 3.49 on the album version and proceeds with Jay's lead vocals removed, however instead of fading out at this point as the album version would have done, this version jumps to the start of the first verse (beginning at 0.29 on the album version) There is another section with the lead vocals removed, starting at 4.04, before the track comes to a premature halt with a flurry of echoing drums. Following this, the chorus reemerges once more and the song repeats to fade.

A further track was released on *Lost Masters 2 – The Final Cut*:

'Rules Of The Game (Dead Ending Version)' (Warren Bacall)
I only saw one TV performance where a dead-end version of 'Rules Of The Game' was used, and that was the *Little And Large Show* on 17 December 1983. Timed at 3.44, this mix is shorter than the 7" version but longer than the dead-end version used in that show.

These three tracks appeared on *Up Until Now (The 30th Anniversary Hits Collection)*:

'London Town (TV Mix)' (Andy Hill)
An admirable but quickly recorded version of 'London Town' made for television, divested of Andy Hill's production, Ian Bairnson's solo (there are no guitars at all on this track) and very heavy on the synthesisers. It is nice to hear as an alternative arrangement, but I can't imagine anyone choosing this version in preference to its studio counterpart.

'Rules Of The Game (TV Mix)' (Warren Bacall)
Another version rerecorded for television. The keyboard melody that precedes the verses is dispensed with, and this mix, as would be expected, lacks the power and urgency of the studio version. It is worth seeking out for Fizz fans, though, as this mix is longer than the single release on account of the song unexpectedly going into a reggae rhythm at the 3.45 mark, presumably after the TV broadcast would have faded out.

'When We Were Young (TV Mix)' (Warren Bacall)
A rendition of the group's ninth single, complete with a dead ending. As with all TV mixes, this does not come anywhere close to the studio version, and some of the finer musical touches are either simplified or omitted.

I Hear Talk (1984)

Personnel:
Mike Nolan: lead vocals, backing vocals
Cheryl Baker: lead vocals, backing vocals
Bobby G: lead vocals, backing vocals
Jay Aston: lead vocals, backing vocals
Andy Hill: keyboards, guitars, bass
Simon Darlow: keyboards
Billy Livsey: keyboards
Richard Cottle: keyboards
Tobias Boshell: keyboards
Nick Glennie Smith: keyboards
Graham Broad: drums and percussion
Charles Morgan: drums and percussion
Bob Jenkins: percussion
Ian Bairnson: guitars
Terry Britten: guitars, bass
Pip Williams: guitars
John Read: bass
Gary Twigg: bass
Peter Toms: trombone
Luke Tunney: trumpet
Martin Dobson: saxophone
Peter Woodroffe: Fairlight programmer
Recorded at Power Play Studio, Zurich; Comforts Place Studio, Surrey; Mayfair Recording Studios, London; RAK Studios, London, between 1983 and 1984
Producer: Andy Hill, Brian Tench, Terry Britten, Bobby G
'She Cries' mixed by Brian Tench
Engineers: Trevor Vallis, Martyn Webster, John Hudson, Brian Tench, Simon Sullivan, G. Jackman
Tape op: Mike Ging
Art direction and design: Shoot That Tiger!
Photography: Simon Fowler
UK release date: November 1984
Charts: UK: 66

The group had been working towards releasing their fourth album at the end of 1983, but the *Greatest Hits* album had moved those plans to the spring of 1984. 'Invisible' had been planned as a single, then disregarded. 'Oh Suzanne' had been included as an exclusive track on *Greatest Hits,* and 'Rules Of The Game', 'London Town' and 'When We Were Young' had all been swallowed up by the compilation album. However you look at it, that is a lot of strong material to lose from your forthcoming album.

In March 1984, the group announced a huge UK tour, starting on 3 May and ending on 23 June. It was an ambitious and suitably Orwellian-themed show that is fondly remembered by fans to this day. That same month, the group's fan club stated that 'the new album, which we thought would be out in spring, will not be out until later in the year.' In and around rehearsals and the tour itself, recording sessions for the new album continued. Bucks Fizz had a hold on a new Terry Britten/Graham Lyle song called 'What's Love Got To Do With It', which the group's management relinquished at the request of Terry Britten when Tina Turner wanted to record it. In June 1984, the group recorded two songs with producer Pip Williams. A cover of Nik Kershaw's 'She Cries' was later mixed by Brian Tench and included on the album, whilst the Andy Hill track 'Every Dream Has Broken' was inexplicably consigned to the vaults, where it remained for over two decades.

Three tracks recorded at Power Play Studios, Zurich, were integral to the album: 'I Hear Talk', 'Breaking Me Up' and 'Talking In Your Sleep', with the latter released as the lead single from the album in August 1984. It displayed a more guitar-driven AOR sound, and it restored Bucks Fizz to the UK top 20, reaching number 15. The follow-up single was another cover version, 'Golden Days', which was produced by Terry Britten but stalled just outside the top 40 at number 42.

I Hear Talk arrived in November 1984 and received a muted response, peaking at number 66, the group's lowest charting album at this point. The reviews at the time were equally lukewarm, although *Record Mirror* were savage, awarding the album one star and stating, 'Same old bill of fare from the codgers you've heard at least 100 times before.' For some fans, it is their favourite Bucks Fizz album, and from its cover to its contents, this is a mature record with some great vocals and great arrangements. It is also a moodier collection that moved the group away from upbeat material and embraced lyrics that were sombre or even dark. For me, this album has some stellar moments, but it also feels like the group's least cohesive collection; the two Andy Hill/Warren Bacall tracks seem like the remains of the album the group were making in late 1983, whilst the three tracks recorded in Switzerland symbolise the direction the group were heading in. 'Golden Days' and 'She Cries' are fine songs, and Bucks Fizz did great versions of both of them, but given the wealth of excellent original material the group had recorded in the 18 months since *Hand Cut*, the inclusion of three cover versions on one album seemed unnecessary. *I Hear Talk* was reissued on CD for the first time 20 years later, with the inclusion of selected B-sides, 12" bonus tracks and later material recorded in 1988. In 2006 and 2008, *The Lost Masters* and *Lost Masters 2 – The Final Cut* unearthed a wealth of unreleased alternate and extended versions from this period.

Far more seriously, on 11 December 1984, the group were touring the UK in support of the album when they were involved in a coach crash. They had just played a concert at Newcastle City Hall and had boarded the coach to head to the Gosforth Park Hotel. The A1 heading into Newcastle had roadworks, so traffic had to be diverted onto one side of the road when normally it would be a dual carriageway. The group's coach collided with an articulated lorry; 14 people were injured, including all four members of the group. The group's keyboard player, Tom Marshall, was placed in intensive care at Newcastle Royal Victoria Infirmary, and Cheryl and Mike, who were at the front of the coach at the time, went through the windscreen. The quote below is from Cheryl Baker on the *Life Stories* podcast, who says it far more powerfully and poignantly than I could ever hope to:

> I woke up in the road. I don't remember a thing about it, nor does Mike; we both went through the windscreen … The first thing I did was to move my legs, to make sure that I could. I broke three vertebrae in my back, and because I had a little mini skirt on and a pair of boots, I took all the skin off one leg and off my back, so when I went to the hospital, they had to put a cradle over me so that nothing touched me. The next morning in the hospital, Mike came in to see me. We both looked a terrible mess … I was bruised all over, I had a black eye, I'd put my tooth through my bottom lip, my hair looked like I'd backcombed it with blood and glass, as did Mike. I said, 'Oh Mike, if your fans could see you now!' and he replied, 'Don't make me laugh. I've got a terrible headache.' And he slipped into a coma shortly after that. He had to have a blood clot removed from his brain, which changed him completely.

'I Hear Talk' (Andy Hill/Pete Sinfield)
Released as a single in December 1984. Chart place: UK: 34
A wonderful track but a bold way to open the album as 'I Hear Talk' does not set out to immediately grab your attention, rather it begins with just a drum machine, bass, guitar and keyboards, and slowly builds into a superb pop rock track. The lyrics centre on problems in a relationship fuelled by rumours and hearsay, with the lines 'Chinese whispers circulate/There's a newsman leaning on your garden gate' implying that what is overheard can be misrepresented to create headlines. As ever, Pete Sinfield addresses the subject in a poetic way and 'So when it's all wrapped up like it's meant to be/The only trap that's left is jealousy' remains a great line to include in a pop song. There is an assurance to Andy Hill's production, and he shapes the song by not bringing in the drums until the first chorus and adding a brass section that accentuates the guitar and keyboard melodies, making the chorus sound bigger. Listen out, too, for the little touches that all add to the song, such as Bobby's wordless vocal preceding the first verse, Mike's supportive backing vocals during the second verse, the shift in the rhythm during the middle eight and the echoing 'talk' harmonies that appear at the start and end of the song and before the second verse.

Bobby sings lead on this track, but he shares vocal duties with Cheryl, who joins him on the latter part of each verse, whilst Cheryl sings the

'Chinese whispers circulate' middle eight alone. It is very different from tracks like 'Rules Of The Game' released a year earlier, or even this album's lead single, 'Talking In Your Sleep', so it took me by surprise initially, but it is a superb, sophisticated track that stands up today as one of the group's best songs.

The song was remixed and scheduled for a single release in December 1984 when the group were involved in the coach crash. RCA went ahead with the proposed release date of the single, although with members of the group hospitalised and Mike fighting for his life, there was absolutely no possibility of promoting it beyond airplay, a promotional video and a variety of single formats. 'I Hear Talk' charted at number 34 in the UK. The 7" featured a non-album track, 'Pulling Me Under', written, produced and sung by Bobby. The 12" single featured an extended mix of 'I Hear Talk' and a bonus track, 'Invisible', which had originally been planned as the follow-up to 'When We Were Young' in 1983. In addition to the standard 7", there is also a limited edition with a 1985 calendar poster.

Advertisements for the 7" and 12" singles, prior to the accident, advertised the TV shows that Bucks Fizz would be appearing on. The group's appearance on *Hogmanay* on BBC1 on New Year's Eve was obviously impossible, but two pre-recorded performances of 'I Hear Talk' went ahead: *Pebble Mill At One* on 4 January 1985 and *Razzmatazz* on 9 January 1985 (Episode 96). Bucks Fizz had also filmed a promotional video for the song shortly before the crash. It frames the song as a story inside a snow globe, with Bobby moving through a winter landscape, seeing Cheryl's face on magazine covers and imagining he sees her in a crowd. Jay and Mike portray a number of seemingly incidental characters that contrive to bring them together at the end. It is skilfully done, and you should know that I absolutely stole Bobby's look in this video at the time.

In 1985, this song was edited and reworked by Disconet and found a home in US dance clubs, which in turn led to Trevor Vallis remixing the song. His remix was included on some versions of the group's next album, *Writing On The Wall*. Additionally, Venezuelan singer Melissa, who previously had scored a hit in Latin America with her Spanish-language recording of 'Getting Kinda Lonely', covered this song in 1986 under the title 'A Volar'. It was included on her album *III*, and her video for the song can be found online.

'Indebted To You' (Andy Hill/Warren Bacall)

The *I Hear Talk* album cover is quite a sombre one; a black sleeve with a sepia-toned picture of the group, taken at Camber Sands in East Sussex, featuring three of the members looking away and only Bobby looking towards the camera. In some ways, the cover is indicative of its contents as it quickly becomes apparent that, more than any other Bucks Fizz album, *I Hear Talk* has a distinct mood to it, occasionally wistful, but often more than a little dark. 'Indebted To You' is a case in point. It is a great track and one of the highlights of the album, but Andy Hill and Warren Bacall's song of an intense and emotionally damaging love is hardly cheery stuff.

A rolling piano sound gradually fades in, setting the mood for the song, before a keyboard motif emerges. This phrase repeats throughout the song, playing continuously at the beginning and end and throughout each chorus, with the drums, bass and guitars all revolving around it. Bobby sings the lead, but the delivery is slightly disorienting, with his voice double-tracked and additional vocals stressing individual words, often at the start or end of each line. The lyrics are actually quite bitter, expressing gratitude towards someone for changing them in not entirely positive ways: 'With you, I really learned how to cry/I'm indebted to you/You showed me how to lie'. Even the guitar solo is unusual, fading in over Cheryl's vocals and consisting of just six notes with a sustained final one merging back into the song like a howl. For the final chorus, everything is stripped away except for the vocals, drums and that constant keyboard refrain. When the instrumentation returns, the chorus is never repeated, as Bobby's solo voice and Cheryl's harmonies simply repeat the words of the title. The keyboard phrase that introduced the song continues to dominate, with Ian Bairnson's guitar solo in the background in the final few bars as the song fades out.

It is an extraordinary track and, not for the first or last time, light years away from their Eurovision beginnings. And yet, as good as this version of 'Indebted To You' is, it emerged 24 years later that an even better version of the song had remained unreleased for over two decades.

'Tears On The Ballroom Floor' (Anthony Phillips/Roy Hill)
Fancy another link between progressive rock and Bucks Fizz? Then look no further than this song. Anthony Phillips was the original lead guitarist in Genesis and featured on their albums *From Genesis To Revelation* (1969) and *Trespass* (1970) before releasing his delicately beautiful debut solo album, *The Geese And The Ghost,* in 1977. The song's co-writer, Roy Hill, released his self-titled debut album in 1978 and toured as support to Styx and The Strawbs, briefly replacing Dave Cousins in the latter. In 1983 and 1984, he wrote several songs with Anthony Phillips, including this one. Shortly afterwards, Roy Hill teamed up with Strawbs' bassist Chas Cronk to form a new band, called Cry No More, who subsequently recorded their own different versions of 'Tears On the Ballroom Floor'. It was released on their album *Smile* in 1986 (on Cold Harbour Records) and again in 1987 when a David Richards-produced version was lifted as a single from their eponymous album on Parlophone.

This Bucks Fizz version is produced by Brian Tench, his first solo production for the group, which gives the song a harder and more synthesised feel than an Andy Hill production. Although Graham Broad and Ian Bairnson are credited with drums and guitar, respectively, no one plays bass, and it is Simon Darlow and Billy Livesey's keyboards that dominate.

Sandwiched between two songs about relationships that have become decidedly toxic, 'Tears On The Ballroom Floor' comes as a bit of light relief. Although tinged by sadness, the 'two young lovers' still care for each other, their tears being a result of their imminent parting, 'for they know the night will be over soon'. Cheryl Baker has her only solo lead vocal of the album on this sweetly poignant track, with Mike Nolan's backing vocals towards the conclusion, mirroring the song's recurring keyboard melody. The track that appeared on *I Hear Talk* was edited down from a slightly longer version that eventually surfaced on *The Lost Masters* in 2006.

'Cold War' (Domenic Bugatti)
Brian Tench produced the track, with Bobby G credited with producing the vocals. Bobby assumes lead vocal duties himself, with Cheryl featuring on backing vocals in the chorus and the latter part of the verses. Musically, a predominantly synth-driven sound gives it a colder, steely edge, and lyrically, we are heading back to despairing terrain once more with a tale of a relationship that has become icy and attritional: a 'Cold War' between two people. 'I've watched my ideals/And my life go down the drain' sings Bobby in the second verse before adding, 'I'd be good for you/If you'd just give peace a shot', but ultimately concluding that a thaw between the couple is unlikely as the chorus repeats 'I don't see an end to the cold war'. It is not one of my favourite tracks by the group, and the despondent lyrics are part of that; however, the subsequent discovery of an extended version (released in 2006) and a 7" mix (released in 2008) suggests that this track, too, may have been considered as a potential single at some stage.

This was the only Bucks Fizz song written by Dominic Bugatti (real name Dominic Roy King), who is a hugely prolific and successful songwriter whose many credits, often in collaboration with Frank Musker, include hits by The Babys, Sheena Easton and The Three Degrees. A song the pair wrote for Chaka Khan called 'Fate' was later sampled and became an international dance anthem for Stardust, 'Music Sounds Better With You'. Domenic Bugatti also has a connection with The Fizz, co-writing 'Chain Of Disaster', a 1985 solo single for Bobby McVay.

'Golden Days' (Terry Britten/Sue Shifrin)
Released as a single in October 1984. Chart place: UK: 42
English guitarist, singer-songwriter and record producer Terry Britten had a connection to Cliff Richard stretching right back to the late 1960s. He had been part of Cliff's touring band and played on and contributed songs to several of his albums, most notably 'Devil Woman', which in 1976 had given Cliff his first UK top ten single in three years. Terry also contributed original material to *Every Face Tells A Story,* the Gospel album *Small Corners* and *Green Light*. In 1979, he produced Cliff Richard's *Rock N Roll Juvenile* album, writing ten of its 12 songs whilst developing a successful songwriting

collaboration with B. A. Robertson. This resulted in Terry Britten creating hits for Cliff Richard with 'Hot Shot' and the brilliant, enigmatic 'Carrie' (one of Cliff Richard's finest singles in my opinion), but also a string of top 20 hits for B.A. Robertson with 'Bang Bang', 'Knocked It Off', 'Kool In The Kaftan' and 'To Be Or Not To Be'.

Following the success of 'We Don't Talk Anymore', Cliff worked with songwriter Alan Tarney for his next record, 1980's *I'm No Hero* (as a footnote, an early Andy Hill track called 'Give A Little Bit More' is featured on this album) whilst Terry Britten began writing with Sue Shifrin, contributing 'Love Make Me Strong' to Olivia Newton-John's *Physical* album and writing two excellent singles for Hank Marvin with 'Don't Talk' and 'The Trouble With Me Is You'. When Cliff Richard released his 25th anniversary album, *Silver,* in 1983, it included three songs by Terry Britten and Sue Shifrin: 'Never Say Die (Give A Little Bit More)', the lead single from the album, which Terry Britten also produced, a cover version of 'Hold On', originally recorded by Kirsty McNichol, and 'The Golden Days Are Over'.

The lyrics of the track are quite solemn, telling the story of a faded movie star recalling halcyon days when she was feted and adored, but now, 'There's no more silver screen/Just another broken dream'. The Cliff Richard version, produced by Craig Pruess, is quite spacious with a dramatic string arrangement, conjuring up images of a spectral figure haunting a movie sound stage. By contrast, the Bucks Fizz version, produced by Terry Britten, is smaller in scale and feels darker and more claustrophobic in its tone, perhaps more accurately capturing the lyrics and evoking a reclusive figure replaying scenes of her former glories in her mind. Bobby sings lead on the verses, but the vocals are more of a group affair, with Mike featured prominently in the chorus and Jay, Cheryl and Mike each given their own lines towards the end of the song.

The track was released as a single in October 1984, but it failed to capitalise on the success of 'Talking In Your Sleep' and stalled just outside the top 40 at number 42. The 7" featured a Cheryl Baker song, 'Where Do I Go Now', as the B-side, whilst a 7" picture disc added a 'Rock Medley' recorded at Glasgow Apollo. The 12" did not feature an extended version (although one would be created in 2008), but it did include an exclusive track, 'One Touch Too Much'.

Offsetting the sad lyrics, the promotional video was a mostly humorous one. It depicts the group as 1920s silent movie stars with Jay as the damsel in distress, Mike hamming it up delightfully as the villain who ties Jay to the railway track, then runs away, Cheryl being adorable as a 1920s flapper girl and Bobby in driving goggles, shaking his fist as he chases after Mike in the final scene. The silent movie is intercut with colour shots of the group in a projection room, being mobbed by fans at a stage door, and Cheryl in a black dress and veil portraying the secluded movie star. A dead-end mix was prepared for a performance of the song on *Wogan* (this mix later appeared instead of the single version on *The Very Best Of Bucks Fizz*), whilst a TV mix was used for an appearance on *Sunday Sunday.*

Support for the single came from *Classic Rock* co-founder Dave Ling, who wrote in *Number One* magazine, 'They've been consistent hitmakers for years and 'Golden Days' looks set to score highly for them once again. The sultry lead vocal is backed up by the usual perfect three-part harmonies and a chorus you won't get rid of for days. Great stuff.' I would agree that 'Golden Days' is an excellent song, and the Bucks Fizz version is arguably better than, or at least equal to, the Cliff Richard version, but I am not convinced that this was the best choice for a single. *Silver* was a very strong album by Cliff Richard with a number of excellent album tracks, including 'Love Stealer' (which Bucks Fizz performed on their 1984 tour), 'Locked Inside Your Prison' and 'Silver's Home Tonight'. 'The Golden Days Are Over' was a strong album track among several others, which is where Cliff chose to leave it. After a run of bold single choices, covering a Cliff Richard album track seemed an unusually cautious move, and I think there were stronger and more adventurous options amongst the group's original material. I know a lot of Bucks Fizz fans love this song, and I do too, but I think it should have remained as an album track.

'Talking In Your Sleep' (Jimmy Marinos/Wally Palmar/Mike Skill/Coz Canler/Peter Solley)

Released as a single in August 1984. Chart place: UK: 15

'Talking In Your Sleep' was originally released by American rock band The Romantics in 1983. It became the band's most successful single in the US, climbing to number three in the *Billboard* Hot 100 and hovering there for three consecutive weeks during January and February 1984 – denied a top two slot by Culture Club's 'Karma Chameleon', 'Owner Of A Lonely Heart' by Yes (both of which were number one singles) and later 'Joanna' by Kool and The Gang. It featured on the group's fourth album, *In Heat,* but neither the single nor the album by The Romantics charted in the UK. The Bucks Fizz version was released in August 1984 and was the lead single from *I Hear Talk.* It was the first single the group had released in nine months and became their tenth top 20 hit, reaching number 15.

The Romantics' version was a fine guitar-based pop rock song, built around a relentless big beat, Mike Skill's bass riff and two electric guitar rhythms. The Bucks Fizz version changed the arrangement, bookending the song with atmospheric, robotic keyboards, dispensing with one of the guitar parts, using keyboards to play the other, and beefing up the main riff considerably with Andy Hill (bass) and Ian Bairnson (guitar) playing in unison. I have heard it argued that the Bucks Fizz version is 'lost' without those two guitar parts, but for me, and possibly this is because I heard the Fizz version first, these parts were a distraction and the song was leaner and more impactful without them. Whatever your views, 'Talking In Your Sleep' undoubtedly demonstrated a shift towards an AOR sound for Bucks Fizz, accompanied by a revelation that Bobby possessed a voice ideally suited to the group's more rock-oriented material.

The respective videos displayed a difference, too. The Romantics' version, shown widely on MTV at the time, cut performance footage of the group with images of young women dressed in lingerie and night attire, all standing in rows with their eyes closed. The Bucks Fizz version framed the group members in the windows of a building on a sweltering summer evening before they each escaped to the rooftop, where a small mysterious figure interacts with the group. It was fun to watch and, as Cheryl Baker remarked in the sleeve notes to *The Very Best Of Bucks Fizz,* 'The video was fun to make, although I'll never be sure of the bouncing alien!' In a 1984 interview with *Look In,* Bobby expressed his hopes for the new single:

> I'm very enthusiastic about this one. What happened in the past was that we tended to just sling records out. It was mostly down to the record company, though: we had a lot of material recorded, and if there's something there, the record company will put it out, regardless of what you want. What we did was not give them any material for a long time. So now we've got to the stage where we're doing what we want to do, as opposed to being pressurised by them.

The group's first TV performance of their new single was on a prime-time BBC Saturday evening variety show called *The Main Attraction* on Saturday 18 August 1984, and it immediately marked a change in how Bucks Fizz presented themselves visually, with Bobby and Mike both brandishing guitars: Bobby, stage right, on bass and Mike, stage left, on electric guitar. It was a look that continued for all mimed TV performances up to, and including, 'You And Your Heart So Blue', and although it would vary occasionally thereafter, it was rare that you would see Bobby or Mike without a musical instrument on the group's TV performances from this point on. This included the group's return to *Top Of The Pops* on 30 August 1984 (Episode 1067). This show was transmitted live and incorporated the naming of a new British Rail Inter City express train, and an attempt to break the existing record for the fastest time from London Paddington to Bristol Temple Meads. Unfortunately for Bucks Fizz, the train arrived in Bristol ('going like the clappers' in the words of Simon Bates) right in the middle of their performance, which was cut during the second verse as the live show went to an outside broadcast. It worked in the group's favour, though, as they were invited back to *Top Of The Pops* the following week (Episode 1068) to open the show, by which time the record had climbed 13 places to number 21.

The single was issued in 7" and 12" formats. The 12" featured an extended version of the A-side, whilst both formats featured a new song, 'Don't Think You're Fooling Me', written and produced by Bobby. A limited-edition 7" EP with a gatefold sleeve followed shortly afterwards and included two live tracks, 'Twentieth Century Hero' and 'Don't Pay the Ferryman', recorded at the Glasgow Apollo on their tour earlier that year.

'Breaking Me Up' (Andy Hill/Frank Musker)
In my opinion, this should have been a single. Master tapes salvaged two decades later revealed the existence of a 7" mix and an extended version, so that possibility seems to have been considered. Andy Hill had been collaborating with Frank Musker since 1983, writing 'My Girl And Me', which was released as a single by Chris Norman with Hill producing, but this was their only co-write on a Bucks Fizz track. 'Breaking Me Up' is a punchy, rock-oriented song and the natural, home-grown successor to 'Talking In Your Sleep'. It is a song that you could have dropped unannounced into Radio One's *The Friday Rock Show* at the time without raising too many eyebrows, and it is one of many songs I want to play to people who think that 'Making Your Mind Up' is all that Bucks Fizz have to offer.

After a number of downbeat songs on the first half of the album, this track and the preceding one feel like a catharsis. The song is powered by Ian Bairnson's guitar riff with Bobby, once again, providing an outstanding lead vocal and the group adding harmonies on the song's killer hook line. 'Breaking Me Up' somehow made it to the B-side of 'I Hear Talk' when it was released in Canada, but I cannot help wondering why this track was never released in the US. Alongside their British pop contemporaries, and purveyors of commercial rock such as Night Ranger, Animotion and John Parr, all of whom were on the *Billboard* charts around that time, I think this track could have found a home. It would at least have been worth a try.

Almost 40 years later, this track was the subject of a faithful but excellent cover version by Swedish melodic rock band Emotional Fire, who recorded it as part of their 2023 mini album *Will You Be There*.

'January's Gone' (Andy Hill/Ian Bairnson)
Speaking to Radio Luxembourg in January 1985, Bobby described 'January's Gone' as 'one of those songs we've been wanting to record for quite a long time'. If there was a gap between the writing of this song and the recording of it, then all I can say is that it was worth the wait. Mike Nolan is blessed with a beautiful melodic voice, and this lovely song highlights that brilliantly. The group harmonies in the second half of the verses and in the chorus are stunning, with Cheryl in particular deserving all the flowers for her lovely harmonies, which support Mike's lead vocal so perfectly. The drum sound on the track is intentionally compressed and flat-sounding, allowing the vocals and banks of keyboards to carry the song. The guitar is quiet in the mix, only rising to the surface during the chorus, playing a rhythmic phrase alongside the vocals.

Sequenced after two guitar-heavy pop-rock songs, 'January's Gone' is a moment of calm, and its tale of reminiscence and wistful longing for a lost love renders it lyrically unlike anything else on the album. Beyond the singles, there are a number of Bucks Fizz 'deep cuts' deserving of wider recognition, or at least radio play, and 'January's Gone' is definitely one of them. It is a delightful and underappreciated song.

'She Cries' (Nik Kershaw)
In an interview with Bucks Fizz in *Number One* magazine in 1984, Peter Martin suggested that the group's forthcoming album 'might feature a specially written Nik Kershaw track'. In the end, it was a cover version of 'She Cries', the B-side of 'Dancing Girls', the third single lifted from Nik's superb debut album *Human Racing*.

The Bucks Fizz version was produced by Pip Williams, whose long and successful career began as a session musician in the early 1970s before moving on to production, most notably a trilogy of classic Status Quo albums, *Rockin' All Over The World* (1977), *If You Can't Stand The Heat* (1978) and *Whatever You Want* (1979), and later The Moody Blues on *Long Distance Voyager* (1981) and *The Present* (1983).

It appears that this track was recorded in the summer of 1984, but not mixed. The producer of each track on *I Hear Talk* is credited on the album sleeve, but this song carries an additional credit that reads 'mixed by Brian Tench'. A version of 'She Cries' on *The Lost Masters* years later demonstrates that there was a lot more on the multi-tracks that could potentially have been used, making Brian Tench's mix on this track seem even more sparse in retrospect. However, the lush-sounding version of 'She Cries' on *The Lost Masters* would have sounded incongruous in this context, and Brian Tench's mix seems to suit the mood of this sometimes bleak and downbeat album. Once more, Bobby is the lead vocalist, with group harmonies on the chorus and Mike adding a melodic vocal on the 'my, my don't you cry' lyrics between the chorus and the second verse. It is a typically intelligent song by Nik Kershaw, but lyrically it leads the album back towards darker territory with its observation of a woman whose beauty commands attention and who is seemingly assured, self-contained, even disdainful, but hides a sadness behind that façade.

'Thief In The Night' (Andy Hill/Warren Bacall)
Previous Bucks Fizz albums had ended with a happy, uplifting song, but *I Hear Talk* offered no such consolation. 'Thief In The Night' is a compelling track, with the group's harmonies creating an ominous, haunting soundscape. The song begins with a lone echoing piano followed by a wall of disquieting harmonies and electronic sound that, to me, always seemed to mimic rainfall, before both give way to a heavy drumbeat. Brian Tench produces the song, and once again, he brings a harder edge to the sound with electronic drums (Graham Broad) and keyboards (Richard Cottle and Andy Hill), the only instruments. There is no softness or warmth here, only a cold, impervious sound that mirrors the nature of the 'thief' in the song title. Jay, finally, has her moment in the spotlight on the album, and once again, she takes a Warren Bacall song and delivers a wonderfully dramatic, theatrical vocal.

Following the second chorus, there is an instrumental break with atmospheric keyboards and a brief return of the piano from the song's introduction, all of which stops abruptly with a vocal section by Bobby, Mike and Cheryl. Bobby and Mike's multitracked voices are unusually deep and a little foreboding, whilst Cheryl's repeated calls of 'cry' escalate in pitch and intensity, with a haunting final 'cry' evoking the 'cry in the night' of the song's lyrics as it fades back into the chorus. It is unusual, a little perturbing, and I had not heard Bucks Fizz use their voices in this way on a track before.

It is a great way to end the album and, along with 'Invisible', 'Oh Suzanne', 'Indebted To You', 'London Town' and 'Rules Of The Game', is perhaps indicative of the direction the album could have taken if it had been released in May 1984, as was originally planned. Tommy Vance declared 'Thief In The Night' to be 'one of my favourite tracks' by the group. Personally, I like this track, but it is a dark and disconcerting one. Following the group's dreadful coach crash in December 1984, I found it hard to listen to, and it was about a year before I could go back to the song and enjoy it.

Surprisingly, 'Thief In The Night' was reintroduced to the group's live setlist in 1986 when it became a solo number for Shelley Preston.

Bonus Tracks

These two tracks were added to *Hand Cut: The Definitive Edition* CD:

'Don't Pay The Ferryman (Live)' (Chris de Burgh)

Originally recorded by Chris de Burgh, this was the lead single from his 1982 album *The Getaway* and became his first UK hit single, reaching number 48. It was one of several cover versions performed by Bucks Fizz during their 1984 tour that were often used as showcases for individual members. This track was recorded at the Apollo, Glasgow, on 11 May 1984, not 4 March 1983 as stated on the 2004 BMG reissue of *Are You Ready* and 2015's *Hand Cut: The Definitive Edition*. Although Bucks Fizz played Glasgow Apollo on that date, neither this song nor '20th Century Hero' was part of the group's setlist for the 1983 tour. Mike and Bobby perform this song with the band and it first appeared on the limited edition *Talking In Your Sleep* EP.

'20th Century Hero (Live)' (Andy Hill/Pete Sinfield)

Originally from 1982's *Are You Ready*, this live version was also recorded at the Apollo in Glasgow on 11 May 1984. The song appeared third in the group's set between 'London Town' and a cover version of Cliff Richard's 'Love Stealer' performed by Mike. This live track first appeared on the *Talking In Your Sleep* EP and later as the B-side to the 1989 single release of 'You Love Love'.

These 19 tracks were added to *I Hear Talk: The Definitive Edition* CD:

'Don't Think You're Fooling Me' (Bobby G)

This track originally appeared on the B-side to 'Talking In Your Sleep'. It was written and produced by Bobby, who provides lead and backing vocals, with

Cheryl adding backing vocals and a vocal part that precedes each verse. Whilst this is definitely B-side material, it is a pleasant, catchy song with keyboards and electronic drums being the only instruments.

'Where Do I Go Now' (Cheryl Baker)
It was a pleasant surprise to see a song credited to Cheryl Baker as the B-side to 'Golden Days'. Cheryl produced the track with Adrian Sheppard and Richard Cottle, who, along with Mike Nolan, are the only ones to feature on this song. It is a pleasing mid-tempo ballad, with Richard Cottle's keyboards shaping the track and providing a fine solo halfway through the song. Lyrically, it concerns the uncertainty of moving on from a relationship, knowing that it is the right thing to do, but still loving the other person despite it all. Sadly, this was the first and last Bucks Fizz song written solely by Cheryl, but it is a lovely one.

'One Touch Too Much' (Andy Hill/Sue Shifrin)
A synth-driven number that was originally a bonus track on the 'Golden Days' 12" single. A bright, lively and melodic keyboard intro gets the song off to a terrific start, but the keyboard-only instrumentation from this point on becomes a little robotic and I find myself thinking that bass and electric guitar, along with additional percussion, might lend the song more power and feeling and frame Cheryl's vocals more effectively. The following year, this song became the debut single for Swedish pop duo Katz and featured on their only album, *Female Of The Species*.

'Pulling Me Under' (Bobby G)
This track was written and produced by Bobby, who is the only member of the group singing on it, rendering it a Bobby G solo track in all but name. It originally appeared on the B-side to 'I Hear Talk'. It is a pleasant song, if a little repetitive, with keyboards and a drum machine being the only instruments.

'Invisible' (Andy Hill/Mike Batt)
In the late summer of 1983, 'Invisible' was announced as the tenth single by Bucks Fizz and the intended follow-up to 'When We Were Young'. Fifteen months later, it was finally released as a bonus track on the 12" of 'I Hear Talk'. Had this song been included on *I Hear Talk*, it would have been one of the standout tracks. If you haven't heard 'Invisible', then put this book down immediately and go and listen to it.

I bought the 12" single of 'I Hear Talk' at the time, knowing the history of this track, and I was beyond excited to hear it. 'Invisible' fully justified all my anticipation. This was the only Bucks Fizz song to feature a co-write credit for Mike Batt but his lyrics here lean more towards the quirky, abstract style of his 1982 audio visual piece *Zero Zero* as they describe love as a compelling, sometimes destructive force, but also as something intangible that cannot be seen or defined ('You say you're looking for love/ How do you know when it's here?').

Musically, 'Invisible' takes 'When We Were Young' as a starting point and then leaps off in another direction to create a dark, dramatic, exciting and fabulous pop song. Once again, Jay is featured on lead vocals and she delivers a spirited, powerhouse vocal, but it is also worth appreciating for Cheryl's glorious harmonies, which are all over this track. Warren Bacall's 'When We Were Young' had taken Bucks Fizz in a heavier direction, but that song was primarily based around keyboards and a huge drum sound. As the proposed follow-up, 'Invisible' continued in a heavier style but was much more of a guitar-based song. There are no guitar solos here, but there is an excellent riff at the 2.58 mark, with Cheryl's 'Love is invisible' vocal line over the top of it, and this is very much an 'air guitar' moment.

For me, 'Invisible' was recorded at an exciting and creative time for the group, and whilst I was grateful to have heard it many months later, I couldn't help but lament what seemed a waste of a brilliant track. It could have been a single, it should have been on the album and it is definitely one of the many hidden treasures in the Bucks Fizz catalogue.

'Evil Man' (Jay Aston)
A bonus track on the 'You And Your Heart So Blue' 12" single. Apart from the sleeve of the German 12" single, which credited Jay as producer, this song was billed simply as 'A Big Note Music Production'. Jay is the only vocalist on this track, which is hampered by a thin electronic drum sound and a mix that diminishes Jay's powerful vocals, especially during the final chorus.

'I Hear Talk (7" Mix)' (Andy Hill/Pete Sinfield)
A punchy remix with the drums more prominent and some minor alterations to the vocals and brass section. This mix is surprisingly overlooked in favour of the album version on several compilations.

'I Hear Talk (Disconet Remix)' (Andy Hill/Pete Sinfield)
'Disconet' was a label and remix subscription service exclusively for DJs that issued its first release in October 1977. Subscribers to the service would receive extended remixes and exclusive tracks. This track was originally billed as 'I Hear Talk (Re Edit)' and appeared on a Disconet US Promo 12", Volume 7 Program 13, in 1985. Perhaps inspired by the attention this mix received in America, a different extended remix of 'I Hear Talk' was created in 1986 and subsequently included as a track on vinyl and cassette versions of the group's next album, *Writing On The Wall*.

'I Hear Talk (1984 Extended Version)' (Andy Hill/Pete Sinfield)
This extended mix was the one that was featured on the 12" single in 1984. In contrast to later mixes, this one builds slowly, with a largely instrumental first

half of the song, no drums until the 2.12 mark and no lead vocal until Cheryl's 'Chinese whispers circulate' section, occurring three minutes into the track. The latter half of the song features Bobby's lead vocal, an edit after the second chorus and different effects on the vocals.

'Talking In Your Sleep (Extended Version)' (Jimmy Marinos/ Wally Palmar/Mike Skill/Coz Canler/Peter Solley)
The original 12" version showcases a prolonged introduction but rarely features Mike and Bobby's chorus vocals. The chorus vocals at the end, on the lines 'I hear the secrets that you keep/When you're talking in your sleep', are sung with a different rhythm not used on any other version.

'Thief In The Night' (Extended Version)' (Andy Hill/Warren Bacall)
When Dean Murphy was made custodian of the Bucks Fizz master tapes, one of the many delights to be discovered was numerous unreleased extended versions of tracks from *I Hear Talk,* created at the time but placed in storage until they were salvaged, preserved, mastered and released in 2006 on *The Lost Masters* and 2008 on *Lost Masters 2 – The Final Cut*. This mix was one of them. It begins as the album version does, followed by an instrumental section, with Jay's lead vocal on the first verse starting at 2.02. Cheryl's vocal is removed from the section preceding the final chorus to leave just Mike and Bobby. A stripped-back instrumental version of the chorus follows before the mix loops back to the song's piano solo and then proceeds as per the album version.

'Cold War (Extended Version)' (Domenic Bugatti)
Another extended mix, produced in 1984 and released 22 years later on *The Lost Masters*. It begins with a remixed, instrumental version of the first verse and chorus, then edits to the album version of the track at 1.18. There is a further instrumental section after the guitar solo, with the vocals returning at 4.43. This mix and a '7" Version', released later in 2008, feature a dead ending that differs from the album track.

'Invisible (Extended Version)' (Andy Hill/Mike Batt)
The 12" mix for the 1983 single that should have finally surfaced on *The Lost Masters* in 2006. It builds up from keyboards and electric guitars, and the end section following the final chorus is extended further, but in between these points, the song is left intact

'Breaking Me Up (Extended Version)' (Andy Hill/Frank Musker)
The extended part of this mix is at the start, with a reworking of the introduction based around the keyboards and guitar riff. Once the lead vocal starts at 1.50, not many changes are made, apart from a couple of instrumental sections added after each chorus. This was another mix produced at the time that remained unreleased until 2006.

'She Cries (Original Version)' (Nik Kershaw)
Five drumbeats and we are straight into the song on the album version, but this track begins with a harmony-laden introduction based around the chorus melody. This 'original version' of 'She Cries', mixed and completed by Dean Murphy in 2006, is a much grander affair, with more harmonies in the chorus and far more harmonies in the verses. Mike's vocals after the first chorus are repeated, and unlike the album version, which fades out, this track comes to a dead end, as Nik Kershaw's original version does. There is a very strong argument for saying that this mix is better than the one that appeared on *I Hear Talk,* but it would have sounded out of place in that context, and Brian Tench's mix blends in better with the rest of the album.

'Indebted To You (Jay Aston Lead Vocal)' (Andy Hill/Warren Bacall)
One of the thrilling highlights of *Lost Masters 2* was this alternate version of 'Indebted To You' with Jay Aston on lead vocals. All of the things that made the album track so great are present and correct, right down to the off-kilter vocals with the stress in unusual places, but now we are taking it up a level. It is notable that all of the post-*Hand Cut* Warren Bacall songs featured female lead vocals from either Jay or Cheryl, with the version of 'Indebted To You' that appeared on *I Hear Talk* the sole exception. I would argue that Bobby comes into his own on tracks like 'I Hear Talk' or more rock-oriented material like 'Breaking Me Up', but, in this instance, Jay's ability to adopt an affected vocal makes her voice a more natural fit for 'Indebted To You'.

This version features additional harmonies in the second verse and leading up to each chorus. In a variation from the album version, the instrumentation continues during the final chorus, and the song just keeps building. Following this, as with the album track, Cheryl's harmonies and Bobby's solo voice repeat the words of the title, but Bobby's vocals work better on this version for precisely the same reasons that his voice at the end of 'When We Were Young' was so effective, as it acts as a contrast with Jay. This version also extends beyond the album version, coming in at 27 seconds longer, with additional drum fills from Graham Broad as the song fades. The album version is great, but this is better.

'Rock Medley Live (Eye Of The Tiger/Hot Legs/Since You've Been Gone/Heartbreaker/Deadringer For Love/Whatever You Want)'
(Frankie Sullivan/Jim Petrik/Rod Stewart/Russ Ballard/Geoff Gill/Cliff Wade/Jim Steinman/Andy Bown/Richard Parfitt)
A final track taken from the group's performance at Glasgow Apollo on 11 May 1984. It was mixed by Bobby G and was initially exclusive to the 7" picture disc of 'Golden Days' (RCA FIZP3). It was the penultimate song of the night, with 'Land Of Make Believe' as the encore, as 'Making Your Mind Up' formed part of a medley of Bucks Fizz hits performed earlier in the show. The picture disc incorrectly credits 'Heartbreaker' to 'B, M and R Gibb', referencing

the Dionne Warwick song of the same name, but here Cheryl performs the 1979 Pat Benatar track. This would be the last time that Bucks Fizz played the Apollo, Glasgow (tickets in the circle were £4!), as the fondly remembered but run-down venue with its famous 'bouncing balcony' closed its doors for the final time in June 1985.

'Censored' (Andy Hill/Nichola Martin)
'Censored' was the third single by Paris, released in 1982. If you could take the instrumentation from the Paris version and add the four members of Bucks Fizz to it, then you would have a great pop song on your hands. This Brian Tench-produced cover version, which originally appeared on the *You And Your Heart So Blue* EP, is slower and more considered than the Paris version and loses some of the urgency and excitement of the original in the process.

'One Touch (Don't Mean Devotion)' (Andy Hill)
Another track that was originally recorded by Paris, this time as the B-side to 'Have You Ever Been In Love'. This song had potential for Bucks Fizz if it had remained close to the Paris arrangement, kept the intimacy of the vocals and instruments and perhaps been presented as a duet between Bobby and Cheryl with harmonies in the chorus. As it is, the Bucks Fizz version is slower, just over a minute and a half longer, the duet idea is abandoned after the opening verse and it is all a bit plodding by comparison.

This track appeared on the first CD reissue of *Are You Ready* in 2000:

'What's Love Got To Do With It' (Terry Britten/Graham Lyle)
A classic what-might-have-been moment in the Bucks Fizz story. Several months before Tina Turner recorded this song, it had been offered to Bucks Fizz. Jay Aston told the *Celebrity Catch Up* podcast in 2023, 'She (Tina Turner) made a version that was like the original demo, and somehow, through a friend of mine, I heard the demo before we even recorded it.' Cheryl recalls that the producer they were working with insisted the song was written for a male vocal and treated both Jay and her in a patronising way: 'It was awful. I wanted to walk out. He was so condescending.' Jay goes on to describe the Bucks Fizz version as 'Very 1980s. And not in a good way', and it is undeniable that Terry Britten realised the potential of his own song more fully, playing on and producing Tina Turner's much cooler, edgier and definitive rendition. In 2024, Terry Britten told *The Strange Brew* podcast how Tina Turner came to record the song:

> We (Terry Britten and Graham Lyle) did the demo, and then Bucks Fizz heard it. It's a bit of a long-winded story, but when I heard that Tina wanted to do the song and wanted me to produce it, I thought, well, Bucks Fizz

> already had a hold on the song. I knew that Tina wouldn't do it if it was not a brand-new song, so I went and had a chat with the manager, told her the situation, and she said, 'Oh, we'll hold back, no problem. You go ahead and do it.' That was Nichola. She was very good ... I think they did it afterwards, maybe put it out later. I did hear their version, (but) I couldn't actually recognise it as the same song.

Certain songs have a destiny, and they are a combination of the right song, for the right artist, at the right time – I think that is the case here. Tina Turner made the song her own, and it became a US number one single, a huge international hit and scooped up three Grammy awards. The Bucks Fizz version, with Bobby on lead vocals, remained unreleased for 16 years until it appeared on this first CD reissue of *Are You Ready* in 2000. I doubt that Tina Turner's version could ever be bettered, but it is still interesting to ponder what might have happened if only the group could have secured the services of Terry Britten first and let Jay and Cheryl loose on this fantastic song.

These four tracks appeared on *The Lost Masters*:

'Invisible (Early Version)' (Andy Hill/Mike Batt)
This version is the foundation of what 'Invisible' became. As the song developed, there would be additional guitars, keyboards and harmonies. The guitars would become more prominent, some of the vocal lines would change in their delivery and would be higher up in the mix and a section of the song consisting of just percussion, vocals and keyboards had not yet materialised. Even in this early form, though, it is still a great track.

'Indebted To You (Dead End Version)' (Andy Hill/Warren Bacall)
A different mix of the album version. In contrast to the album track, all of the instrumentation continues during the final chorus, at which point the song comes to a dead end.

'Every Dream Has Broken' (Andy Hill)
It is one thing to have great songs hidden away on albums, B-sides or as 12" bonus tracks, but 'Every Dream Has Broken' takes this concept to a whole other level. The track was recorded in June 1984 with Pip Williams producing, but it remained in an unmixed state for over two decades before finally being mixed and completed by Dean Murphy and released on this CD in 2006. It appears not to have been considered for *I Hear Talk,* but it is an outstanding track that would have graced this or any other Bucks Fizz album, so why it wasn't dusted down and mixed for possible inclusion on the group's proposed 1985 album on RCA, or even *Writing On The Wall*, is a bit of a mystery. It has many of the qualities that you would look for in a mid-1980s Bucks Fizz track: a strong lead vocal from Bobby and from Cheryl in the lines

preceding the chorus, an effective hook line and stellar group harmonies in the chorus. All of which is allied to lyrics with a bit of substance that relate to being bereft in the absence of the person that you love. The line 'The tears of a fool go tumbling into the dirt' in the opening verse is a particular favourite. It was an unexpected delight to hear this fully formed track in 2006, 22 years after the group first recorded it.

'Tears On The Ballroom Floor (Long Version)' (Anthony Phillips/Roy Hill)
The version on *I Hear Talk* is an edited version of this mix. Here, the end section of the song is slightly longer, extending the track by 33 seconds, and includes some vocal parts by Cheryl that were cut from the album version.

These seven tracks appeared on *The Lost Masters 2 – The Final Cut*:

'Talking In Your Sleep (Full Unedited Version)' (Jimmy Marinos/Wally Palmar/Mike Skill/Coz Canler/Peter Solley)
The same mix as the album version, but with the length of the second and third choruses doubled. I can see why it was edited down for radio, as the track stops just short of five minutes, but this version is my favourite by virtue of it being slightly longer.

'Breaking Me Up (7" Version)' (Andy Hill/Frank Musker)
A few tweaks to the album version with the keyboards higher in the mix at the expense of the guitars and a tighter, more compressed drum sound. Unusually, it is also longer than the album version, with the chorus repeating at the end more often and some of Bobby's vocal ad-libs falling in different places as a consequence.

'Don't Think You're Fooling Me (Demo)' (Bobby G)
The melody, lyrics and structure of this track are the same as the version released as the B-side to 'Talking In Your Sleep' in 1984, which is essentially a refined version of Bobby's demo. The keyboard parts here are a little more rudimentary, and Bobby sings all the vocal parts himself, including those sung by Cheryl on the record. This version also has fewer harmonies on the chorus and some differences in the vocal phrasing.

'Tears On The Ballroom Floor (The Original Idea)' (Anthony Phillips/Roy Hill)
A gentler rendition of the track with a less pronounced drum sound, additional guitar parts not found on the album version and Bobby and Mike's vocals reduced in the mix. Cheryl's additional vocals from the 'Long Version' are woven into the chorus, and the song comes to a dead end rather than fading out, rendering it slightly longer than the album mix.

'Every Dream Has Broken (Alternate Version)' (Andy Hill)
An alternate mix of the track with the keyboards a little more prominent. The 2006 version also contains a section at 3.11 comprised of just vocals, drums and bass, which is dispensed with here, rendering this version 30 seconds shorter. As a footnote, the sleeve credits this song to Pip Williams rather than Andy Hill.

'Invisible (Early Edit)' (Andy Hill/Mike Batt)
The full-length version of 'Invisible' is just over four and a half minutes long, and this track seems to be an early attempt to edit the end section so that it fits under four minutes. The ending seems abrupt, though, more akin to a dead ending made for a TV performance.

'Cold War (7" Version)' (Domenic Bugatti)
A slightly shorter rendition of the album track with a dead ending, based around the female vocals from the chorus. On the album version, the male vocals in the chorus sing 'And I don't see an end to the cold war' with the female vocals responding, 'Can't see an end to this war', and these two lines repeat to fade. On this 7" version, the male lead vocals stop at 3.20, leaving the female vocals to sing 'Can't see an end/No I can't see an end to this…' with a brief pause before the song concludes with a simultaneous single drum beat, the final chords from Richard Cottle on keyboards and female vocal harmonies. This alternate ending was also utilised on the 'extended version' of the track, first released in 2006.

Writing On The Wall (1986)

Personnel:
Mike Nolan: lead vocals, backing vocals
Cheryl Baker: lead vocals, backing vocals
Bobby G: lead vocals, backing vocals
Shelley Preston: vocals, backing vocals
Andy Hill: keyboards, guitars, bass, drum programming, brass arrangements
Ian Bairnson: guitars
J.J. Bell: guitar
Matthew Cang: guitar
Graham Broad: drums
Tony Beard: drums
Andrew Paresi: drums
Gary Wallis: drums and percussion
Will Parnell: percussion
Robert Lea: percussion
Felix Krish: bass
Steve Price: bass
Danny Choggar: keyboards
Richard Cottle: keyboards
Alan Park: keyboards
Nick Graham: keyboards
Gary Hutchins: keyboards and programming
Bobby G: harmonica
John Thirkell: trumpet
Luke Tunney: trumpet
Peter Toms: trombone
Gary Barnacle: saxophone
Mel Collins: saxophone
Martin Dobson: saxophone
Peter Woodfoffe: Fairlight programming
Original version of 'I Hear Talk' recorded at Power Play Studios, Zurich, in the summer of 1984. Remaining tracks recorded between March 1985 and October 1986. Studios not listed on credits, but include Comforts Place Studios, Surrey.
Producers: Andy Hill, Mike Myers, Trevor Vallis, David Motion, Bobby G
'I Hear Talk' mixed by Trevor Vallis
Engineers: Trevor Vallis, Brian Tench, Peter Woodroffe, Trigger
Art direction: Alwyn Clayden
Design: Green Ink
Photography: Michael Hoppen
Styling: Suzanne Rose
Cheryl's dress: Patricia Lester
Shelley's dress: David Fielden
Bobby: Woodhouse, Source

Mike: Versace
UK release date: November 1986
Charts: UK: 89

> Some of my work I can't listen to, but oddly enough, I find the Bucks Fizz stuff holds up really well: 'You And Your Heart So Blue' I like a lot. 'I Hear Talk' was ahead of its time with the invasion of privacy thing. I like them. I had to write in the style of Bucks Fizz, and they had some great tunes, big productions.
> **Pete Sinfield (*Record Collector,* October 2007)**

Mercifully, Mike Nolan survived the life-threatening injuries he had suffered in December 1984, as did Tom Marshall, although the road to recovery for both of them would inevitably be a long one. For now, all group activities were on hold. Bobby did a number of TV and radio interviews and promoted his solo single, 'Big Deal', which had charted the previous December. Cheryl's bubbly personality had made her a natural fit for the anarchic children's show *How Dare You,* which she had recorded the previous autumn, and in February 1985, she presented Children's ITV, followed by a series on London Weekend Television called *The Saturday Six O'clock Show,* all of which became the start of a flourishing TV career for her. In the meantime, Mike was unhappy about preventing the others from working and offered to quit the group, as he told *TV Times* in June 1985:

> They told me I needed eight to 12 months off work, but I had three other people to think of. A group can't afford to be out of action that long … and at one point, I wanted to quit, but the others wouldn't let me. They said they wouldn't go on without me, and they'd wait. At the time, I got uptight about it. It made me feel I had to get myself together faster than I wanted.

In an interview with Radio Lancashire in December 1986, Mike said that he had asked the group's management to find work for them, in spite of their understandable reluctance to do so. 'When I started back at work, the hospital said to me, 'You must not go back', but as far as I was concerned, it was my decision … I just said (to the group's management), 'Look, I want to work. It's got nothing to do with the hospital. We all need to work again." In March 1985, the group flew to Mauritius to film a TV special (which would remain unaired, although the footage apparently still exists) with Cheryl telling *TV Times,* 'When we first got there, Mike wandered about like a convalescent. But gradually, he shook it off, became involved in what we were doing and, by the end of our stay, he was much better.' In March 1985, the group also began work on a new track entitled 'You And Your Heart So Blue'.

The next few months were eventful ones. On 18 May 1985, the group appeared on *The Keith Harris Show* performing a lip-synced version of 'Now Those Days Are Gone', their first TV appearance since the coach crash. Even more amazingly, in late May, the group returned to the stage, playing a series of live dates at Birmingham Night Out and Baileys, Watford, which seemed astonishing given the events of the previous December, and made national news. The group signed a sponsorship deal with Sharp Electronics, which led to a series of magazine adverts and 'You And Your Heart So Blue' was radically reworked from a lilting reggae tune sung by Cheryl into a thumping AOR track with Bobby on lead vocal. It was scheduled for single release on 14 June 1985, and the group had recorded a performance for *Razzmatazz,* which was due for broadcast on 12 June. However, on 10 June 1985, Jay, who by her own admission had been unhappy in the group for some time, announced that she was leaving Bucks Fizz. It is not a subject for this book, but her departure, and the tabloid headlines and litigation that followed, is a desperately sad part of the Bucks Fizz story.

Auditions for Jay's replacement were held at The Prince Of Wales Theatre in London, with Shelley Preston, who had little professional singing experience beyond performing in a hotel in Sri Lanka, beating out thousands of other hopefuls to become the new member of Bucks Fizz. She was undeniably thrown straight into things, from being told that she was a member of Bucks Fizz on Monday 1 July 1985, to being interviewed live on national television by Terry Wogan on 3 July and then performing with the group. From that point on, Shelley had photo shoots, interviews and just six weeks to learn the group's songs, harmonies and routines in readiness for the group's *Magical Tour,* which began with a charity performance at Newcastle City Hall on 17 August 1985. She did it, and she did it brilliantly. In an article in *Look In* magazine in October 1985, Mike said, 'As soon as I set eyes on Shelley, I knew she'd be right for the group. Everything about her was so exactly what we were looking for that she just stood right out from the others, and as we went on whittling the numbers down, she looked better and better.' Cheryl would later remark that she took Shelley under her wing and that she was '21 going on fifteen.' That is a lovely description, as there was an adorable, happy, unaffected quality to Shelley that made her impossible not to warm to. As the tour progressed, 'Magical' was released as a single in September 1985. Speaking to Radio South about the tour, Cheryl said, 'We have an album out in October, so there will be a couple of tracks from that'. However, the intended October album did not materialise, and the two tracks Cheryl referred to, 'I Used To Love The Radio' and 'Love In A World Gone Mad', would remain unreleased for now.

It would be eight months until the group's next single, by which time Bucks Fizz had moved to Polydor Records. Discussing the change to *Pop, Rock And Puzzles,* Bobby said:

> RCA had gone through a lot of staff changes, and they didn't seem as interested in us as they used to be. They weren't putting the same effort behind us. We only had a year of the contract to run, so by mutual

agreement, we decided to move to Polydor, who came up with the best deal of all the labels that were interested in signing us.

Bucks Fizz and Polydor came roaring out of the blocks in May 1986 with 'New Beginning', the first single to feature Shelley and a top ten hit in the UK. Two further singles followed, 'Love The One You're With' in August 1986 and 'Keep Each Other Warm' in November 1986. The group's fifth album was also released in November 1986 and included the three Polydor singles, 'You And Your Heart So Blue', 'Magical' and the previously unreleased 'Love In A World Gone Mad' from the proposed October 1985 RCA album and a further three new songs (or four if you had the UK CD version). The album fared poorly, which it did not deserve, peaking at number 89 and managing only one week on the chart. The 1986 *Not Quite Christmas Tour* was another matter entirely and was hugely successful, beginning at the now defunct Golddiggers in Chippenham at the start of December, and culminating with a sold-out show at the London Palladium on 21 December 1986.

Reviews of the album at the time were mixed. *Number One* bizarrely gave credit to songs that were 'all lush strings and harmonies' (there are no strings on this album) but added that 'for the most part, Bobby, Cheryl, Shelley and Mike give a fair impression of American AOR rockers – in the most melodic way possible, of course.' Tom Hibbert in *Smash Hits* awarded the album 8 out of 10, describing it as 'thoroughly ravishing, proper popular music' and 'awesomely brilliantly conceived pop music performed with relish.'

There is no definitive version of *Writing On The Wall* as the original vinyl, cassette and CD versions all have a slightly different track listing and running order. In 2004, a single CD 'Special Edition' was issued, which omitted all of the tracks recorded for RCA. In 2012, a 2CD 'Ultimate Edition' was issued with another different running order but again including only the Polydor material. Reviewing the 2012 reissue for *Music News,* Paul Chapinal commented, 'This isn't a lost classic, it's an album by a band trying to catch up, found wanting and losing their identity. This album failed miserably when it was first released and has been pretty much forgotten until now.' Not by me, it hasn't. For me, *Writing On The Wall* was an album that ticked all the boxes. I loved the direction that the group were going in with their singles in 1985 – 'New Beginning' is stupendous – and the album includes the full-length version of 'Keep Each Other Warm'. 'Love In A World Gone Mad' had finally escaped from captivity, 'Soul Motion' was great live and is immense fun and the other new tracks all hit the spot. This album came at a happy time for me and added to that happiness, so I have nothing but positive feelings about it.

'New Beginning (Mamba Seyra)' (Mike Myers/Tony Gibber)

Released as a single in May 1986. Chart place: UK: 8

There was fierce competition in the UK singles charts in the summer of 1986: Madonna had just released 'Papa Don't Preach' as the second single from her forthcoming album *True Blue,* Wham! brought down the curtain on a peerless pop career with the glorious 'Edge Of Heaven' and great records like 'Sledgehammer' (Peter Gabriel), 'Addicted To Love' (Robert Palmer), 'I Can't Wait' (Nu Shooz), 'Set Me Free' (Jaki Graham) 'Venus' (Bananarama) and 'Happy Hour' (The Housemartins) were vying for top ten places. In an ideal world, however, 'New Beginning' would have had its moment at the top of the charts. It is a thunderous pop epic with a massive production, huge choral vocals and a joyful, optimistic message. It was also quite literally a new beginning for the group: their first single on a new record label (Polydor), their first single to feature Shelley and, as it turned out, their biggest hit since 1982.

'New Beginning' was a cover version of a song initially released by Force 8 in May 1985. That version is sometimes referred to as 'The Dooleys under an assumed name' but the vocals and the reverse of the picture sleeve of that version suggest that it's a hybrid of the Liverpool dance group Force 8 (Neil Danns, David Danns, James Welsh and Kevin Duala), Vicki Roe (who joined The Dooleys following the departure of Helen Dooley) and Val Tuffnel, with Mike Myers producing. It is quite possible that members of The Dooleys may have added instrumentation and vocals, given Vicki Roe's association with the group and Mike Myers' long-standing relationship with them. The original is a fine track with a synthesised, Hi-NRG feel and provides the template for the Bucks Fizz version; however, Andy Hill, in conjunction with Mike Myers, who is credited as co-producer on this track, builds it into something monumental, with layers of percussion and hundreds of voices that sound like an entire community coming together to celebrate.

In the sleeve notes to *The Very Best Of Bucks Fizz,* Cheryl describes the recording of the track as 'hard, fun and ridiculous!' as, in addition to the group repeatedly multi-tracking their own vocals, there was also a children's choir, a gospel choir and a track that utilised everyone who happened to be in the studio at the time. After a number of singles that featured one member of the group as lead singer, 'New Beginning' returned the group to the style of two boys, two girls alternating lines, which had resulted in the group's biggest commercial successes. It also marked a change in mood after a number of songs with more sombre lyrical themes and an unashamed return to pop after heading towards melodic rock territory with their two previous singles, 'You And Your Heart So Blue' and 'Magical'. Shelley put it beautifully, speaking to Radio Hallam in November 1986:

> We wanted to come back with something that would really knock people out. From 'I Hear Talk' to 'Magical', the sound had progressed; it had got a bit heavier. We wanted to go back a bit, but keep that heavier sound, and 'New Beginning' seemed to match the two. Going back to the two boys/two girls format, but (with) all that heavy percussion and a very strong bass line. It seemed to work.

It undoubtedly did work, returning the group to the UK top ten for the first time since 1983 and becoming a top 40 hit in Ireland, Belgium and the Netherlands. As a fan, I felt happy for them and proud of them. The pop music press of the time were less enthused; *Smash Hits* handed their single reviews over to Tony James and Martin Degville of Sigue Sigue Sputnik, who were dismissive of it, whilst a young Paul Bursche writing in *Number One* magazine gave it two stars, concluding, 'I still think it would be a nicer world if they stuck to hosting TV shows and flogging compact discs, but that's life.'

The single was released in a picture sleeve with a new track, 'In Your Eyes', as the B-side. Some copies came with a poster bag (Polydor POSPG 794). A 7" picture disc was also available, with or without a poster (Polydor POSPP 594). There were two main 12" singles: the first (Polydor POSPX 794) featured an extended version of the A-side and included an additional track, 'I Need Your Love'. A second 12" (Polydor POSPA 794) carried the 'Ian Levine Remix' on the A-side. A dub version of the Ian Levine mix was available on the B-side of the UK 12" promo (Polydor FIZZX 1) or on US 12" import copies (Polydor 885 274-1).

The group performed the song on *Wogan* on 2 June 1986 and *Razzmatazz* on 11 June 1986 (Episode 115), which also featured an interview with Shelley. At that time, Saturday mornings were brightened by Cheryl co-presenting *The Saturday Picture Show* with Mark Curry, and Bucks Fizz appeared as guests on the programme on 31 May 1986. The promotional video appeared as a 'top 40 breaker' on *Top Of The Pops* on 11 June 1986, and the group returned to open the show on 18 June 1986 (Episode 1162). It would be their final appearance on *Top Of The Pops,* although the promotional video was shown two weeks later (Episode 1164).

'You And Your Heart So Blue' (Andy Hill/Pete Sinfield)
Released as a single in June 1985. Chart place: UK: 43
Released on 14 June 1985, this was a magnificent track that came at a pivotal time for the group. Earlier versions of the song were softer and slower, with a lilting reggae rhythm, and featured Cheryl on lead vocals. By the time the single was released, the tempo had sped up considerably, and it had transformed into a guitar-driven rock song with a huge drum sound and an embattled but excellent lead vocal from Bobby. Lyrically, it is the story of a relationship and deals with the frustration yet acceptance of loving someone with everything that you have, only for it not to be enough for them. Ian Bairnson's guitars and Tony Beard's drums are all over this track, with Bobby singing the verses and the group harmonising on the chorus. The middle eight section with the drums and Cheryl's prominent multi-tracked vocals is a fabulous moment in an already great song. However, despite its powerful sound and anthemic chorus, this is actually a bittersweet song that keeps slipping into a minor key to evoke that mood.

The group filmed a performance of the song for *Razzmatazz,* which was broadcast on 12 June 1985 (Episode 110). It was to be the only TV performance of the song with Jay, who had left the group by the time the episode was broadcast. A subsequent promotional video featured only Bobby, Cheryl and Mike, and the group were interviewed on several TV shows to promote the song. The single had peaked at number 43 in the UK and was already on its way down the charts when an adorably sweet and visibly nervous Shelley Preston was unveiled as the new member of Bucks Fizz live on *Wogan* on Wednesday 3 July (Season 5, Episode 58), having only been told that she was a member of the group two days previously. 'Welcome to Bucks Fizz', said host Terry Wogan, 'Welcome to the new Bucks Fizz.' For me, it is this song, and specifically this performance, where the Shelley Preston era of Bucks Fizz begins, and I was delighted when this track was included on the album.

The 7" single featured 'Now Those Days Are Gone' on the B-side, whilst a limited edition four-track EP (RCA PB 40233 (E)) was housed in a different sleeve and featured a competition to win one of 25 Sharp personal hifi systems. It also contained two exclusive tracks: 'Censored' and 'One Touch (Don't Mean Devotion)', both originally recorded by Paris. There were two 12" versions, both of which featured 'Evil Man', a track written and performed by Jay. The first 12" contained the single version of 'You And Your Heart So Blue' whilst the second one (RCA PT 40234 R) featured a 'special extended remix' by Andy Hill.

I would love to tell you that the pop music press were kind, but sadly, they weren't. Max Bell, writing in *Number One,* said, 'I must say I always detested Bucks Fizz. Those medallion men! And those girls! Yucksville. Their records have always exemplified the worst traits of British pop kitsch. This is no exception.' Mike Gardner, writing in *Record Mirror,* described it as 'a spirited version of the sort of thing Smokie used to knock out in their sleep.' My view is that 'You And Your Heart So Blue' is a belter of a track, and it featured in the group's live setlist for their 1985 and 1986 tours. There are also two cover versions worth looking out for. The first is by Amazulu from their 1987 album *Spellbound,* where producer Andy Hill revisits his earlier reggae-style approach to this song, and the second is by The Four Seasons, who covered it on their 1992 album *Hope And Glory.*

'Soul Motion' (Andy Hill/Gary Bell)

When I first played my vinyl copy of *Writing On The Wall* in 1986, I already knew and loved most of the tracks on side one, all of which had previously been released as singles, so I deliberately homed in on the one new song: 'Soul Motion'. Many fans have expressed the opinion that this track should have been released as a single and the follow-up to 'New Beginning' in preference to 'Love The One You're With', and there is some merit to the argument. Notably, unlike the actual follow-up single, 'Soul Motion' formed part of the group's live setlist in 1986 and always went down a storm. Cheryl and Shelley had a choreographed routine for this song, too (which I loved and may have replicated on occasions), that I think would have worked well visually in a promotional video or on a TV show.

This is an energetic, joyous pop song with a lively brass section and a fine lead vocal from Bobby. The lyrics from Gary Bell, who also wrote for Stevie Lange, Five Star and later Cathy Dennis, are playfully sexual, but vague enough to be left open to interpretation. Once again, Andy Hill, aided by engineer Trevor Vallis, goes all out with the production. The track has a huge sound; the multitrack tapes reveal that this song has 92 separate tracks. To that end, I would recommend seeking out Dean Murphy's excellent 2011 extended mix, which does a superb job of highlighting less evident elements of the song, not least the group's layered harmonies.

'Magical' (John Parr/Meatloaf)

Released as a single in September 1985. Chart place: UK: 57

A Bucks Fizz track cowritten by Meat Loaf?! You'd better believe it! Musician, singer and songwriter John Parr had been working with Meat Loaf, contributing two tracks to his 1984 album *Bad Attitude:* 'Cheatin' In Your Dreams' and 'Don't Leave Your Mark On Me', the latter a co-write with Julia Downes. In the same year, 'Magical' was the lead track on John Parr's self-titled debut album. It was released as a single in the US, peaking at number 73 on the *Billboard* charts. The album was reissued in the UK in 1985 on London Records with the inclusion of John Parr's biggest hit, 'St Elmo's Fire (Man In Motion)', which was a US number one, a top ten hit in the UK and a song that Bucks Fizz would perform themselves as part of their 'Rock Medley' during their *Not Quite Christmas Tour* in 1986.

The John Parr track is great, and the Bucks Fizz rendition is quite similar (drummer Graham Broad played on both versions), but for me, Bucks Fizz have the edge. The guitar chords on the John Parr track are more abrasive, but Ian Bairnson steals it here with an excellent solo towards the end of the song, complemented by some funky bass guitar from Felix Krish. What really lifts the song, though, are the vocals. Bobby excels once again on a more rock-oriented track, and the backing vocals (again including an uncredited Andy Hill) lend it a rich, full sound, whilst Cheryl Baker's vocals on the 'heat, flame, embers' section are a magical touch.

The single received a negative review in *Smash Hits,* whilst *Number One* remarked that the song 'sounds like the Power Station on a five-amp fuse' before adding, 'Magical is not an apt title.' Praise came from a surprising source, however, when *Kerrang!* (yes, you read that right!) reviewer Derek Oliver said:

> Late summer madness? The Fizz turn heavy metal? Absolutely! Written by John Parr and subsequently tossed around and then sat on by the beast of burden, Meat Loaf, 'Magical' is an exceptional indication that behind those four plastic smiles lies real savvy! Indeed, this is redolent of the work that

> some of our more well-respected hard rock artists are currently wrestling with in order to gain stardom … Excellent.

For an encore, the magazine reviewed the group's show at London Dominion on 26 September 1985 in their following issue (number 105).

I thought 'Magical' was excellent, a natural extension of records like 'Talking In Your Sleep' and 'Breaking Me Up', but it was not a commercially successful move for Bucks Fizz, and it became their joint lowest charting single, peaking at number 57. Plans for an album of the same name were shelved, and 'Magical' was one of a number of tracks held over for what became the *Writing On The Wall* album. Although she did not feature on the recording itself, 'Magical' was significant as it was the first single released with Shelley Preston as an official member of the group. She was featured on the single's picture sleeve and the subsequent radio and TV appearances to promote the single. At the time of the single's release, Bucks Fizz were in the middle of their *Magical Tour,* which began with a charity performance at Newcastle City Hall on 17 August 1985 and ended at Blackpool Opera House on 5 October 1985 – a show I attended.

The single was released on 7" and 12" with a picture sleeve and the magnificent 'Oh Suzanne' as the B-side. The 12" included Andy Hill's extended remix of 'You And Your Heart So Blue' for those who may have missed it the first time around. There was no promotional video for the single and few TV performances, although an interview and a performance of the song in the grounds of the Pebble Mill studios in Edgbaston for *Pebble Mill At One* can currently be found online.

'Keep Each Other Warm (Long Version)' (Andy Hill/Pete Sinfield)

Released as a single in November 1986. Chart place: UK: 45

I was fortunate enough to attend the last night of the *Not Quite Christmas Tour* at the London Palladium in 1986, and to this day, it was one of the best atmospheres at a pop concert that I have ever experienced. In an excellent review of the show in *Number One* magazine, Jacqui Carter wrote:

> They (Bucks Fizz) clearly enjoyed themselves on stage and made sure that their fans were having a good time, too. It's good to see people swamped in scarves and swaying to and fro, and I felt like I was seeing the last of a dying breed.

I was one of those people (I still have the scarf), and when I read her review, I instantly knew that she was referring to the audience during 'Keep Each Other Warm'. Released as a single just ahead of the tour and the album, it is a gorgeous ballad with a huge chorus and a romantic lyric that can also be interpreted as referring to the protective love and safe harbour of family or friends. *Smash Hits* predicted 'Bucks Fizz will find themselves back amongst the yule with a very welcome hit.' Sadly, it wasn't to be, although it deserved much better; the single met a similar fate to its predecessor, stalling just outside the top 40 and peaking at number 45.

There were three versions of this song at the time: an edited 7" single version, which fades out just past the four-minute mark, a shorter version with a cold ending that was used for TV performances and the 'Long Version' featured on the 12" single. I was delighted when the long version was included on *Writing On The Wall,* and although I appreciate that a five and a half minute long single might be a bit much for TV and radio, I really wish that this were the version that most people had heard.

'Keep Each Other Warm' is a song that gradually builds. The first verse features a solo vocal from Bobby, the second verse (cut from the 7" version) introduces harmony parts, most prominently from Bobby and Cheryl, with additional layers of harmonies added from all of the group, building up to the chorus. Throughout it all, the only instrumentation is Andy Hill's keyboards. At the start of the second verse, drums (Gary Wallis) and guitar (J.J. Bell) kick in, and the song settles into a groove (picture a sold-out crowd at the London Palladium swaying at this point) before the harmonies come back bigger and stronger for the song's second chorus. A key change and a soaring Mel Collins saxophone solo elevate the song as, on the single version, the chorus repeats to fade, but this long version still has one magical moment left. For the final moments of the song, it all quietens down again until it is just the keyboards once more with gorgeous female vocal harmonies. I remember playing this song for the first time in 1986 when I bought the 12" single, and it was a spine-tingling moment, and even now it still affects me that way sometimes.

The promotional video features Bucks Fizz in a house performing the song, intercut with scenes emphasising the song's lyrics – a young girl cradling a doll on a wind-battered street, a shepherd in search of a lost sheep – that Bobby and Shelley are seemingly viewing through the windows. The group also performed the song on the prime-time Sunday evening show, *Live From The Piccadilly,* on 2 November 1986, ahead of the single's release. In addition to the 7" and 12" versions, there was also a 12" picture disc to collect (Polydor POSPP 835) and a limited-edition double pack 7" edition, which included a free single featuring the 'Writing On The Wall Medley' containing extracts of all ten tracks from the forthcoming album.

In 1989, Barry Manilow would record the track for his self-titled album. He also released it as a single in America, and although it didn't break into the main *Billboard* chart, his version, featuring a string section and a choir, reached number seven on the Adult Contemporary chart.

'Love The One You're With' (Stephen Stills)

Released as a single in August 1986. Chart place: UK: 47

This song was written by the legendary American musician, singer and songwriter Stephen Stills, who, by his mid-20s, had already achieved huge success and international acclaim with Buffalo Springfield, Crosby, Stills & Nash and later Crosby, Stills, Nash & Young. 'Love The One You're With' was released as the lead single from his debut solo album in 1970. It was not a massive hit single in the UK, peaking at number 37 in 1971, but it became an instant classic and was a top 20 hit in America twice in quick succession, first for Stills himself, reaching number 14, and then for The Isley Brothers, who charted at number 18. For his version, Stephen Stills enlisted the help of Rita Coolidge, her sister Priscilla Jones, John Sebastian and his fellow bandmates David Crosby and Graham Nash to sing backing vocals. In his memoir, *Wild Tales,* Graham Nash explained how the song came about:

> I happen to love that song. Stephen got the title from Billy Preston, who was playing with The Beatles at the time. They were at Stephen's house in Surrey, hanging with Ringo (Starr). Apparently, Stephen spotted some girl and made a comment to Billy about how great she was. Billy responded, 'Hey man, if you can't be with the one you love, love the one you're with.' To which Stephen replied, 'Excuse me, can I borrow a pen?'

In the sleeve notes to the *CSN* CD box set, Stephen Stills confirms this, stating, 'The title came from a party with Billy Preston. I asked him if I could pinch this line he had, and he said, 'Sure.' So, I took the phrase and wrote a song around it.' In an interview on *TVAM* in 1986, Mike Nolan was asked about the 'free love' inferences in the lyrics and responded: 'I don't think it really means what it says. It's just a way of telling everybody that, no matter what, love everybody.'

Whether this should have been the follow-up single to 'New Beginning' is debatable. 1986 had been a good year for cover versions of late 1960s/early 1970s songs, with 'Eloise' (The Damned), 'Venus' (Bananarama) and 'Spirit In The Sky' (Doctor and the Medics) having already become top ten hits. Sadly, Bucks Fizz were less successful, with the single peaking at number 47. In an interview with Red Rose Radio in 1986, Mike revealed that the group had doubts about releasing the track as a single:

> None of us really wanted to go with it, but the record company were so convinced that we would have a hit with this following 'New Beginning'. The four of us never believed that because you have a hit record … there is no problem with a follow-up. There are problems. And I was, without a doubt, right, so was Shelley, so was Cheryl. Bobby liked it, but he wasn't sure about it being a single.

In the same interview, Shelley concurred:

> With 'New Beginning', we went in and recorded it, and we thought, 'Yeah! This is the one. This is the record we have been waiting to do to get back in

the charts.' We went and did 'Love The One You're With', and we all thought 'It's alright', but we all got that feeling that it wasn't going to do the same as 'New Beginning'.

However, if the golden rule of a cover version is to do it better or do it differently, then I would argue that, musically speaking, Bucks Fizz succeeded. Their take on the song featured thumping, programmed drums, Felix Krish and Andy Hill on bass and guitars and an energetic 1980s dance pop feel, complete with joyous harmony vocals from the Fizz themselves. I knew and loved the original, but I loved what Bucks Fizz chose to do with it, and I was happy with that (if not its lowly chart position). As Stephen Stills himself said of his composition, 'It's a good times song, just a bit of fun', and the Bucks Fizz version was undeniably that: a burst of pop positivity in the late summer of 1986.

The promotional video is an unusual one for Bucks Fizz as it displays them in a band setting with a keyboard player, a bass player, three drummers and Mike and Bobby both on electric guitar. It is great to see Shelley featured more prominently, and although I knew that Bobby was not really playing the guitar solo on the track, it is still fun to watch. The group also performed the song on ITV's *Hold Tight* in September 1986 and on *Cheggers Plays Pop* on 12 September (Episode 73).

There were two 7" singles with slightly different picture sleeves: the original release (Polydor POSP 813) and a second one (Polydor POSPC 813) which contained details of a competition to win a Sharp CD/Radio/Cassette player. It's worth noting that the version of 'Love The One You're With' on the album, and what is sometimes referred to on CD reissues as the 7" version, differs from initial 7" vinyl pressings, which start instrumentally, rather than with the vocal refrain from the chorus as is the case with the album version. There were also two 12" singles, one featuring an 'Extended Version' timed at 7.52 (Polydor POSPX 813) and a limited edition 12" (Polydor POSPA 813) with a 'Dance Edit' that ran to 5.08. Each 12" single included a different mix of 'I Hear Talk' and the non-album track 'Too Hard'.

'Love In A World Gone Mad' (Pete Sinfield/Billy Livesey)
One of two brand new songs premiered during the group's *Magical Tour* in 1985. Throughout the tour, the song was performed by Cheryl and Shelley, who alternated lines during the verses, but this version, recorded in 1985, features only Cheryl on lead vocals. It is a delightful little song about holding on to love in a turbulent and uncertain world, and was co-written by musician, songwriter and producer Billy Livesey. Billy's career stretches right back to the early 1970s, and as a musician, his credits include Gallagher and Lyle, Gerry Rafferty, Cliff Richard and Tina Turner. He had previously cowritten Sheena Easton's 'Are You Man Enough' with Graham Lyle, scored a top 20 hit with Shakin' Stevens' 'Give Me Your Heart Tonight' and had

cowritten and produced 'System Addict', which had become a top five hit for Five Star. Just prior to the release of *Writing On The Wall,* he had teamed up with this song's other writer, Pete Sinfield, to create 'Rain Or Shine', another top ten hit for the group, which he also produced.

This track is produced by David Motion, formerly of techno-pop band Home Service, who, earlier in 1985, had produced the eponymous album by Strawberry Switchblade. His production style suits the song admirably, with a compressed drum sound and a harder sound from the keyboards and guitars, which gives the song an 1980s synth pop feel and contrasts with Cheryl's gentle vocals in the verses and the song's sensitive subject matter. The song was briefly considered as a single following the album's release, leading to the only TV performance of the track on *The Little And Large Show* on 28 March 1987.

Interestingly, throughout their *Not Quite Christmas Tour* in 1986, Cheryl and Shelley continued to perform this song together, with Cheryl singing the first verse and Shelley the second. Subsequent CD reissues of *Writing On The Wall* have revealed that Bucks Fizz rerecorded the track in this fashion in 1986, and the existence of a 7" version, an extended 12" mix and a demo featuring Shelley on lead vocals indicate that presenting the song with the lead vocals shared between Cheryl and Shelley in a similar manner to the 1986 live version seems to have been seriously considered. The song also received a blessing from pop royalty when ABBA's Agnetha Faltskog covered the track on her 1987 album *I Stand Alone,* with Peter Cetera producing.

'Don't Turn Back' (Ian Bairnson/Bobby G)
This is the track that is often overlooked on the album, as it is the only one that was not a hit for Bucks Fizz, a hit for another artist or performed live by the group. However, Shelley declared 'Don't Turn Back' to be one of her favourites on the album at the time, and the lyric is a call for resilience and determination in the face of adversity or self-doubt. There is a laid-back groove to this one, with guitars (J.J. Bell and co-writer Ian Bairnson) and keyboards (Richard Cottle) tastefully filling the gaps. Bobby is the lead vocalist, and he gives the track a slick, polished production, making excellent use of a brass section, particularly during the chorus and for a solo spot at the mid-point of the song.

'The Company You Keep' (Bobby G/Steve Glen/Mike Burns)
The only lead vocal by Mike Nolan on the album, but once again, it is a lovely one. Mike has a solo vocal on the first four lines of each verse before being joined, primarily by Cheryl and Shelley, on the next four lines and the chorus. Bobby does a fine job with the production, changing the emphasis of the original lyrics so that this finished version is about being in love with, and remaining faithful to, someone who has embarked on an ill-advised romance. Bobby's production also softens the mood of the song, dispensing with the

heavier drum sound on the song's demo and replacing it with lilting percussion and playing harmonica himself during the song's introduction and instrumental break. It all acts to place the melody and the lovely group harmonies at the centre of the song. The fluttering keyboards from Nick Graham as the chorus repeats to fade is also a nice moment.

The song featured in the group's live setlist during the *Not Quite Christmas Tour,* and perhaps more than any other track on *Writing On The Wall,* this one glanced back to the group's debut album. A gentle little song on an album full of singles.

'I Hear Talk (Extended Version)' (Andy Hill/Pete Sinfield)
This extended remix was included on the UK vinyl edition of the album and as a bonus track on the cassette version. It had been released a few months earlier as a bonus track on the 'Love The One You're With (Dance Edit)' 12" single (Polydor POSPA 813). Following the success of a Disconet remix in America, this new extended version of 'I Hear Talk' was created and including it on the vinyl album allowed a sticker on the cover to proclaim, 'Contains six hit singles', which made sense from a marketing viewpoint. However, one of the features of *Writing On The Wall* is that it is effectively two albums merged into one, with tracks recorded for RCA in 1985 for a proposed album ('You And Your Heart So Blue', 'Magical' and 'Love In A World Gone Mad') and later tracks recorded in 1986 for Polydor. The inclusion of this remix added a third element: a reworking of a track from the group's previous album in 1984 that predated Shelley joining the group. It may also have unintentionally conveyed the impression that there was a shortage of strong new material, which certainly was not the case: 'Give A Little Love', 'I Used To Love The Radio' and 'In Your Eyes', to name just three songs.

There is a variation of this album from 2004, *Writing On The Wall – Special Edition,* which omits all of the 1985 RCA material, but includes this remix, and I know some fans prefer this edition. Personally, I like the tracks the group recorded for RCA and welcome their inclusion; for me, this album is stronger because of them, and they are all part of the group's evolution with Shelley. This remix, as good as it is, and as good as the original track is, was not part of that, and I feel like it belongs on a 12" single rather than on the album itself. Having said all of that, this excellent remix is arguably the best one of the track and takes the Disconet edit as a template and improves upon it. Particularly effective is the section at 1.47, comprised of just backing vocals, electronic percussion and the drums high up in the mix, and later Cheryl's solo vocal, which removes the echo found on the 1984 single and album versions.

'Give A Little Love' (Albert Hammond/Diane Warren)
If you bought the UK vinyl version of *Writing On The Wall,* then the last track on side two was the extended remix of 'I Hear Talk'. If you bought the CD or

the European vinyl version, then track ten, following 'The Company You Keep', was this song. It was first recorded by Albert Hammond and Albert West, released as a single in Europe in 1986, and was the lead track on their album *Hammond West*. Their rendition had a reggae rhythm and featured a children's choir. The Bucks Fizz version was released a couple of months later, first appearing as the B-side to 'Keep Each Other Warm' in November 1986.

The Bucks Fizz version is faster than the original, and the reggae beat is downplayed, but it is a vivacious and good-spirited pop song with Andy Hill's twangy guitar giving it a slight country feel in places. Cheryl provides a fine lead vocal, initially augmented by Shelley on the first chorus and then by the whole group. Following the second chorus, there is a delightful harmony part, with Shelley again featured prominently, starting with the lines 'If everybody took somebody by the hand' before the song returns to the chorus. Once again, it was a case of another great pop song by Bucks Fizz that was hidden in plain sight. Unless you had flipped over the vinyl single of 'Keep Each Other Warm', heard the CD version or had a European vinyl copy of the album, then it's unlikely you would have heard this track. A pity, as it deserved to be included on the cassette version of the album, too, at the very least.

Prior to Bucks Fizz, the song was covered by Ziggy Marley and The Melody Makers and featured on their 1986 album *Hey World!,* but the UK hit version of this song came two years later when Aswad released it as the follow-up to their number one single 'Don't Turn Around'. The positive message of the lyrics suited their chilled-out style and took them to number 11 in the UK charts.

Bonus Tracks

These ten tracks were released on *Writing On The Wall – Special Edition* (2004):

'New Beginning (Previously Unreleased Full-Length Version)' (Mike Myers/Tony Gibber)

The same mix as the album version, but adding an additional part following the 'Historia Futuro' drum break to extend the track from 4.08 to 4.41. This section would be included in remixed form in the song's extended 12" mixes.

'Love The One You're With (Dance Edit)' (Stephen Stills)

This second 12" mix is an edited, rearranged and more compact version of the original 12" single. It begins with the drums, percussion and guitar breakdown from the original extended version, but then returns to the first verse and proceeds with a remixed version of the standard track, restoring Ian Bairnson's guitar solo, which was omitted from the first 12" version. The instrumental version of the third verse, featuring Shelley and Cheryl's backing vocals, is retained before a final edit that cuts to the album version.

'Keep Each Other Warm (7" Version)' (Andy Hill/Pete Sinfield)
A truncated version of the album track that appeared on the 7" single and on side one of the original cassette versions of *Writing On The Wall* (the 'Long Version' was included as a bonus on side two). This mix edits out the second verse and fades the song out early.

'Love In A World Gone Mad (1986 New Version)' (Pete Sinfield/Billy Livesey)
The version of this song on the original album was recorded for RCA Records in 1985 and featured Cheryl on lead vocals. The 2004 *Writing On The Wall Special Edition* replaced it with this 1986 reworking of the track, which the *2012 Ultimate Edition* credited to being produced by the song's co-writer, Billy Livesey. The verses here are a completely different vocal take with Cheryl singing the first verse and Shelley singing the second, with harmonies in the lines leading up to the chorus. The ethereal female vocals in the background during the guitar solo are also a lovely addition to the track. The end of the song fades out, rather than coming to a dead end as the original version does, and there are notable musical changes, too, with additional keyboards, a more natural drum sound and a bass guitar part.

This song was planned as a single, and this 1986 rendition seems to have been produced with that in mind before the idea was shelved and the track became another one consigned to the vaults. It is a pity, as it's a lovely version of the track and it would have made a good single.

'In Your Eyes' (Andy Hill/Warren Bacall)
Originally appearing as the B-side to 'New Beginning', this was the last original Bucks Fizz song to be co-written by Warren Bacall, and typically, the lyrics are darker than other Bucks Fizz songs from this period. The jagged guitar refrain and unusual rhythm have echoes of 'Indebted To You', but Andy Hill's production gives this song a much lighter tone. Cheryl is the lead vocalist on this track, and after a number of 7" B-sides that were either older songs or keyboard-heavy tracks featuring one or two group members, it was refreshing to hear a new one that sounded like a group again, complete with drums, bass, guitar, keyboards and a brass section. A good song, though perhaps not in keeping with the overall mood of the album.

'Too Hard' (Ian Bairnson/Bobby G)
With their forthcoming album *Writing On the Wall* already on its fifth single and a stronger Ian Bairnson/Bobby G song ('Don't Turn Back') ahead of it in the queue, 'Too Hard' was destined to become the B-side to 'Love The One You're With' in August 1986. It is a solid track, though, with a good lead vocal from Bobby, who also produces the song. Particularly effective is a quieter section of the song following the second chorus (beginning at 2.36), which features some lovely harmonies behind Bobby's lead vocal.

'I Need Your Love' (Bobby G)
A tale of someone who walks out on a relationship when things become difficult, but realises that he has made the wrong decision. Effectively, this is a solo track by Bobby, who writes it, produces it and is the only vocalist featured on it. Keyboards and drum machine are the only instruments, with the exception of an electric guitar playing one of the melody lines preceding the first and second verse and a solo after the second chorus. This track first appeared as a bonus on the 'New Beginning' 12" single.

'New Beginning (Mamba Seyra) (Ian Levine Club Mix)' (Mike Myers/Tony Gibber)
Ian Levine was the resident DJ at Blackpool Mecca and later at Heaven nightclub in Charing Cross, London. He was one of the pioneers of Hi-NRG and produced dancefloor classics for Miquel Brown ('So Many Men, So Little Time') and Evelyn Thomas, as well as remixing tracks for Pet Shop Boys, Bronski Beat, Kim Wilde and Hazel Dean. This remix featured on the second 12" and accentuates the female vocals in the chorus and highlights different aspects of the percussion to give it an almost Latin feel in places.

'Love In A World Gone Mad (1986 New Extended Mix)' (Pete Sinfield/Billy Livesey)
A 12" mix of the 1986 version featuring a slow fade-in with Vangelis-like keyboards and group vocals. This gives way to an instrumental version of the chorus, and another one with vocals, before the song loops back to the first verse. The instrumental section is extended and features some indistinct, distorted vocals quietly in the background. Listen out, too, for some additional vocal parts towards the end of the song, not found on the proposed 7" mix.

'New Beginning (Mamba Seyra) (Ian Levine Dub Mix)' (Mike Myers/Tony Gibber)
An engaging and mostly instrumental variation of the Ian Levine Remix. This only appeared on the B-side of the US 12" single (Polydor 885-274-1) or as the B-side of a UK promo 12" single (FIZZX 1).

These eight tracks were released on *Writing On The Wall – The Ultimate Edition* (2012):

'Don't Turn Back (Unedited Version)' (Ian Bairnson/Bobby G)
A longer version of the album track, featuring an additional bass note at the start of the song and continuing beyond the point that the album version fades out to extend the song by 40 seconds.

'Give A Little Love (Unedited Version)' (Albert Hammond/Diane Warren)

Very similar to the 'Long Version' that first appeared on the 12" of 'Keep Each Other Warm' and later on the bonus disc of *The Ultimate Anthology*. The main difference is a vocal part leading up to the chorus at the 2.12 mark that was cut from both the 7" and 12" mixes.

'Love The One You're With (Extended Version)' (Stephen Stills)
The first of the two 12" singles mixes (Polydor POSPX 813). This also appeared on the original (1986) CD version of the album. Personally, I loved this mix, although it can't quite seem to make up its mind if it is a club mix aimed at the dancefloor or a kind of dub version, especially the section between 4.05 and 6.00 that consists of programmed drums, percussion, guitars, bass and snippets of backing vocals.

'New Beginning (Extended Version)' (Mike Myers/Tony Gibber)
The first 12" single (Polydor POSPX 794) and the extended version that was included as a bonus on the cassette and original CD versions of the album. It is a powerful remix that begins as the 7" version does, but then emphasises a thumping kick drum sound, guitars, keyboards and the choral backing vocals. The percussion drops in occasionally, and Bobby's lead vocal on the first verse doesn't begin until 3.31.

'Love The One You're With (Alternate Mix)' (Stephen Stills)
A variation of the album version that begins with just one of the rhythm guitar parts instead of the vocal introduction. The other significant differences are the removal of the second rhythm guitar part during the first verse and fewer harmony vocals during the guitar solo.

'Keep Each Other Warm (The Original Idea)' (Andy Hill/Pete Sinfield)
A softer version of the track with a different vocal take, a gentle and less prominent keyboard part and more electronic percussion. There is a variation on the vocals as the song transitions from the verse to the chorus, which creates a slightly different melody from the album version. On the album version, the lyrics leading into the first chorus are 'Waiting to catch you when you fall/And we'll stand tall, when we're', followed by the first lines of the chorus: 'Blown by the wind/Torn by the storm'. On the album version, the group harmonise and sustain the note on the word 'tall', with the words 'when we're', using just two notes repeated, acting like a punctuation mark and creating a brief pause before the chorus. On this 'Original Idea', there is an overlapping harmony that repeats the line 'And we'll stand tall' and this is followed by the words 'when we are'. This results in three descending notes at the end of the verse, with the extra syllable removing the pause before the chorus and making it less impactful. This is a pleasant variation, but the original idea was not the best one, and the album version is far more

dynamic. This version also sorely misses the song's beautiful coda, as it consists of electronic percussion repeating to fade.

'Love In A World Gone Mad (Shelley Preston Version)' (Pete Sinfield/ Billy Livesey)
This demo version, produced by Billy Livesey, is different musically and vocally from the 1985 and 1986 versions. It has a softer drum sound, electric guitars are dispensed with entirely, and all vocals are by Shelley. At 2.49, there is a section consisting of just vocals and keyboards before the song returns to the chorus, a device used on the 1985 album version but not on Billy Livesey's own 1986 remake.

'The Company You Keep (Demo)' (Bobby G/Steve Glen/Mike Burns)
An early version of the album track, produced by Steve Glen. Musically, it lacks the finesse of the finished version and consists of just keyboards and a drum machine. This version also features just Bobby on vocals, as opposed to the album track, which featured all of the group and lead vocals from Mike. The melody of the song is present on this demo, but the lyrics would undergo a rewrite, changing the tone to become gentler and more romantic. Compare, for instance, the lines in the demo, which state 'I thought that I could make you happy/There was a time you thought so too/I couldn't believe it when it happened/I want to know why I can't have you' with the lyrics on the album version, which read 'There was a time I thought we'd make it/And that love would see us through/I couldn't believe it when it happened/But I'm not giving up on you'.

These two tracks can be found on *The Ultimate Anthology*:

'You And Your Heart So Blue (Extended Version)' (Andy Hill/Pete Sinfield)
This extended remix by Andy Hill appeared on the second 12" of 'You And Your Heart So Blue', (RCA PT 40234 R) and later the 12" of 'Magical'. It builds up from electric guitar, keyboards and vocals. The vocal harmonies on the word 'you' (that first appear at 3.23 on the album version) are dropped in at intervals throughout this mix, including the introduction, the first verse and the second chorus, sometimes with the vocals on this phrase slowed down slightly, creating an almost plaintive effect. The end of the song is extended, and the vocals from the 'Given all the love you needed…' section after the second chorus are removed. Award yourself five bonus points for each time you hear Bobby's 'shot me down' line from the first verse appear in this mix.

'Give A Little Love (Long Version)' (Albert Hammond/Diane Warren)
Originally featured on the 12" of 'Keep Each Other Warm', though surprisingly not as one of the extended mixes on the cassette version. This features an

extended section at the end of the track and a male vocal part during the chorus, which I rather like, that was cut from the 7" version. It is worth appreciating, too, the harmonies and vocal lines by Bucks Fizz that are only found on their rendition of this song.

These two tracks can be found on *Bucks Fizz (2004 Edition)*:

'Love In A World Gone Mad (Previously Unreleased 1985 Version)' (Pete Sinfield/Billy Livesey)
There is a minor difference from the album version here: a two-second a cappella vocal part from Cheryl Baker at the start of the song.

'I Used To Love The Radio' (Andy Hill)
Another of the new songs that were introduced to the live set for the group's 1985 *Magical Tour*. However, whilst 'Love In A World Gone Mad' deservedly found a home on the *Writing On The Wall* album the following year, 'I Used To Love The Radio' disappeared, only to re-emerge 19 years later on the first reissue of the group's 1981 debut album. This David Motion-produced track features Mike on lead vocals, and the lyrics seem to hint at a nuclear apocalypse and its aftermath: 'We can't go near the water/And nothing seems to grow/But there's static on the radio'. The lyrics later reflect on everyday existence before 'someone pushed the button down'. Maybe it didn't fit lyrically with the album, maybe it was passed over in favour of the admittedly lovely 'The Company You Keep', which also featured Mike on vocals, or perhaps it was never considered. Whatever the reason, it is a fine song that deserved a better fate than being a stray and often forgotten bonus track, and, as with the other material recorded during 1985, it warrants a place in the *Writing On The Wall* pantheon.

These two tracks can be found on *The Lost Masters*:

'You & Your Heart So Blue ('So Blue' Mix)' (Andy Hill/Pete Sinfield)
The sleeve notes state that this track was produced by Andy Hill in March 1985, but was not completed, so this was mixed and finished by Dean Murphy in 2006. Cheryl is the lead vocalist on this slower version of the song with a synthesised, reggae beat. It is completely different to the version that came out in 1985, but the lyrics suit its subdued style, and it is a rewarding and quite emotional experience. Knowing that Jay left the group a few months after this was recorded, I find hearing her vocals in the chorus and her repeating 'so blue' line at the end of the song strangely touching.

'You and Your Heart So Blue (A Cappella Version)' (Andy Hill/Pete Sinfield)
An a cappella version of the 'So Blue Mix', included as a hidden bonus track on disc two.

This track was released on *The Lost Masters 2 – The Final Cut*:

'You And Your Heart So Blue (Andy Hill's Mauritius Mix)' (Andy Hill/ Pete Sinfield)
The slower, reggae-tinged version with Cheryl on lead vocals that was unearthed for *The Lost Masters* is the basis for this track. It differs from the 'So Blue Mix' as it begins with a drum machine and echoing, ambient keyboards, with the reggae rhythm not commencing until the lines 'But roses die and moonlight doesn't last forever', occurring at 0.35. Additionally, Jay's vocals towards the end of the song are absent, and this version fades out.

This track was only available as a limited-edition vinyl single:

'The Writing On The Wall Medley (Parts 1 And 2)' (Ian Bairnson/ Bobby G/Andy Hill/Pete Sinfield/Billy Livesey/John Parr/Meatloaf/ Stephen Stills/Gary Bell/Steve Glen/Mike Burns/Mike Myers/Tony Gibber)
This was a free single included with the limited-edition gatefold 7" issue of 'Keep Each Other Warm'. The additional single was allocated its own catalogue number (FIZZG1), and it is effectively an album sampler, with excerpts of each track segued together. Side one consists of 'Don't Turn Back'/'You And Your Heart So Blue'/'Love In A World Gone Mad'/'Magical'/'Keep Each Other Warm'. Side two features 'Love The One You're With'/'Soul Motion'/'I Hear Talk'/'The Company You Keep'/'New Beginning'. It has not been released on CD to date.

The Story So Far (1988)

UK release date: November 1988
Charts: UK: did not chart
Track listing: 1. 'Heart Of Stone', 2. 'Talking In Your Sleep', 3. '20th Century Hero (Live)', 4. 'One Of Those Nights', 5. 'Now Those Days Are Gone', 6. 'Magical', 7. 'Piece Of The Action', 8. 'The Land Of Make Believe', 9. 'I Hear Talk', 10. 'New Beginning (Mamba Seyra)', 11. 'If You Can't Stand The Heat', 12 'My Camera Never Lies', 13. 'You Love Love' 14. 'Run For Your Life', 15. 'You And Your Heart So Blue', 16. 'London Town', 17. 'Making Your Mind Up', 18. 'Keep Each Other Warm'

1987 was a quiet year for Bucks Fizz. There were a few live dates and TV appearances, most notably a Humanitarian Awards Gala at the Royal Albert Hall, where they performed 'New Beginning' and a live version of 'We Are The World', which saw the group joined by Kim Wilde, Junior and Petula Clark, who also performed at the gala. There were UK TV appearances on *Little And Large* ('Love In A World Gone Mad') and *Miss UK* ('Keep Each Other Warm'), but no new single releases, nor any imminent sign of one. A Cheryl Baker solo album seemed more likely.

The group reconvened for a nationwide tour in August 1988 and were featured in an article penned by Hilary Bonner in the *Daily Mirror* on 20 August 1988, in which the reason for the group's 18-month hiatus was attributed to Bobby. 'I didn't want to stop working, but I didn't have any choice', Mike is quoted as saying, 'Bobby was quite determined.' This was later confirmed by Bobby himself in a group interview with Richard Madeley on *This Morning* to promote the release of 'Heart Of Stone': 'I went off and did my own thing … golf, a lot of snooker, a little bit of writing and things. I just basically wanted a break from what we were doing.' As with Mike, Cheryl indicated in the same interview that this break was not a unanimous group decision: 'We wanted to carry on working, but he (Bobby) wanted to have a break for six months and it extended every month.' In the *Daily Mirror* article, Hilary Bonner mentions that Bucks Fizz had recorded four new songs and quotes the lyrics to 'Young Hearts' when she says, 'The one they hope will become a hit single includes the lines 'Nothing can tear us apart/I knew that from the very start'.' However, 'Young Hearts' was not destined to be a single and would remain unreleased for 16 years. The group's next single saw them return to RCA Records with another song the group had performed on their 1988 tour: 'Heart Of Stone'.

The Story So Far was released on the Stylus record label in November 1988. The 18 tracks were licensed from RCA and Polydor and included 'Heart Of Stone', which was the only new song on the collection. It was a strange compilation as it was neither a definitive collection of all the group's hits (it omitted 'Love The One You're With', 'Golden Days', 'Rules Of The Game' and 'When We Were Young') nor did it stick to just singles due to the inclusion of

'You Love Love' from *Hand Cut* and a previously released live version of '20th Century Hero'.

The album was reviewed by Kate Davies in *Number One* magazine, who gave it four stars, but it also highlighted a naggingly persistent view of Bucks Fizz as an unfashionable group that people liked almost despite themselves: 'Well, what can I say about Bucks Fizz that hasn't been chortled over, dismissed, or scoffed at already? Okay, so in most people's estimation, they're a pretty naff pop band, but give this Greatest Hits LP a spin, and you'll be surprised just how many hits they've had and how many you've secretly bopped along to.' The group toured to support the album in April and May 1989, with RCA releasing two tracks from the compilation, 'You Love, Love' b/w '20th Century Hero (Live)', as a single to coincide with this.

'Heart Of Stone' (Andy Hill/Pete Sinfield)
Released as a single in October 1988. Chart place: UK: 50
In September 1988, I found myself at a Bucks Fizz concert at Kings Nightclub in Birmingham (sadly, the venue was demolished some years ago), which is where I first heard this song. At that point, it had not been released, and it was entitled 'Made Of Stone'. It was one of three new songs the group performed that night that were under consideration as potential singles. I fell in love with this song immediately, and I hoped that if the group released another single, it would be this one.

Bucks Fizz recorded the track at Abbey Road Studios in London, and it became their 20th and last single to chart, reaching number 50 in the UK in November 1988. It deserved so much better, and for me, 'Heart Of Stone' is one of the group's best songs. Pete Sinfield's poetic lyrics exist somewhere between social commentary and private emotions, observing that there are times when you want to be impervious to the pain that loving can cause. Musically, it is an expansive, acoustic AOR track, with Bobby on lead vocal for the first verse but sharing all of the others with Cheryl. There is no chorus as such, just two different melody lines, with Shelley and Mike adding excellent supporting harmonies throughout, and Andy Hill's vocals on the 'lay me down, wash away the sorrow' lines adding an effective contrast. 'Heart Of Stone' is a tremendous, soulful pop-rock song, and it should have been a huge international hit for the group in any sort of just universe.

The single found the group back on RCA Records. The 7" featured another new song, 'Here's Looking At You', on the B-side, and 12" copies added the group's number one hit, 'My Camera Never Lies'. The group performed the song on *Record Breakers,* which Cheryl was co-presenting at that time with the wonderful Roy Castle, and on Cheryl's own show, *Eggs And Baker,* on 29 October 1988, which featured the group as guests. However, the musical style and the worldly-wise lyrics of this song were suited to an older audience, and it is a pity that many who might have warmed to 'Heart Of Stone' either never heard it or might have been inclined to dismiss the song based on their preconceptions of Bucks Fizz. The song had a promotional video, which featured the group walking through the grounds of a country mansion and all looking beautifully elegant during the interior shots at the end of the video.

'Heart Of Stone' had an afterlife when it was covered by Cher in 1989, with Peter Asher producing. I love Cher (why would anyone not?), and although I prefer the Bucks Fizz version of 'Heart Of Stone', it is undeniable that she gave the song to a much bigger audience. Cher made 'Heart Of Stone' the title track of her 19th studio album, which reached number one in Australia and was a top ten album in the UK, Canada, the USA and New Zealand. Cher released 'Heart Of Stone' as a single in the UK, where it charted higher than the Bucks Fizz version (UK: 43), and in the US, where it climbed to number 20, and continued to perform the song on her concert tours well into the new millennium. Many years later, I saw a touring theatre production of *The Cher Show* at Wolverhampton's Grand Theatre. By this time, over three decades had elapsed since the song's release and 'Heart Of Stone' had become incorporated into Cher's stellar body of work, alongside her other classics such as 'Woman's World', 'Believe' and 'If I Could Turn Back Time'. 'Heart Of Stone' was featured in the show, and I couldn't help but smile to myself and think back to where and when I first heard it, an unreleased original song performed by Bucks Fizz at a now-defunct venue in Birmingham.

The group would remix and rework the song themselves in subsequent years, with a 2009 acoustic mix and a later extended version featuring a newly recorded vocal by Cheryl (see Appendix 4).

Bonus Tracks

This track appeared on the first CD reissue of *Bucks Fizz* (2004):

'Heart Of Stone (12" Version)' (Andy Hill/Pete Sinfield)

A slightly extended version of the single with a longer fadeout.

These two tracks appeared on the first CD reissue of *I Hear Talk* (2004):

'Here's Looking At You' (Andy Hill/Pete Sinfield)

From the hymnal introduction consisting of just keyboards and vocals, the song has a looser, unembellished feel and is based around a keyboard and guitar riff played in unison that runs throughout most of the song. The song title might imply conviviality or affection, but Pete Sinfield's lyrics are cynical, remarking upon a dispassionate God who observes the state of the world but does not intervene: 'Living on a small, blue world, your hands held up to heaven/Do you ever get the feeling something's wrong?'. The track originally appeared as the B-side to 'Heart Of Stone', although neither the record sleeve nor the record label itself credited who produced the track. It was listed as a 'Big Note Music' production in the 2004 CD reissue. Bobby excels on lead vocals, and it is great to hear Shelley featured more prominently, too.

As one of the new tracks recorded in 1988, 'Here's Looking At You' is a bit of an oddity. Whilst 'Heart Of Stone', 'Young Hearts' and 'Let's Get Wet' were performed live and created with a view to a possible single release and hopefully achieving another hit for the group, this track – clocking in at five minutes and 50 seconds, with a minute-long keyboard solo and a pessimistic lyric – is resolutely uncommercial and does not appear to have been created with that goal in mind.

'Young Hearts' (Andy Hill)
Recorded in August 1988, this was one of four new songs recorded by Bucks Fizz and was considered a potential single at the time. The group performed the song during their live dates in autumn 1988, although it had been dropped from the set by the following year. For me, the decision not to release 'Young Hearts' as a single was the right one, although not including it on *The Story So Far* or as the flip side to 'You Love, Love' when that was released as a single in 1989 made less sense. The track remained unreleased for 16 years until it first appeared on this CD reissue of *I Hear Talk*. It is a straightforward guitar-driven pop-rock track, with Cheryl on lead vocals and Shelley featuring prominently on backing vocals. The production is credited to Nick Tauber (billed as 'Nicky Tauber' here), who is best known for his work on the early Thin Lizzy albums and later producing Toyah and Marillion. The song has a natural, 'live' sound to it that, apart from the fade-out, is similar to how the group performed it in concert.

These two tracks appeared on *The Lost Masters*:

'Young Hearts (Unreleased Version)' (Andy Hill)
This is a different take on the song, with the drums less prominent and a different, rougher mix on the vocals that features Bobby and Mike more. It sounds like an earlier version of the track coming together, but it isn't as punchy as the version previously released on the 2004 *I Hear Talk* reissue. This version features a guitar part in the verses and some vocal ad-libs towards the end that do not really add very much to the song and were wisely discarded later on in the mixing process.

'Young Hearts (Shelley's Mix)' (Andy Hill)
This is an unfinished, hidden track on disc two. Instrumentally, it is the same as the 'Unreleased Version' on this CD, but the first two verses feature a solo lead vocal from Shelley Preston. It runs out of steam, however, as, once we get past the guitar solo, there are no lead vocals at all, just the backing vocals and some of the vocal ad-libs. If you could take the 2004 mix and add one of Shelley's verses from this version, so that Cheryl and Shelley had a verse each, I think you would probably have the perfect version of 'Young Hearts'.

This track appeared on *The Lost Masters 2 – The Final Cut*:

'Let's Get Wet (Cheryl Baker Lead Vocal)' (Steve Glen/Mike Burns)
Another song recorded in 1988 as a potential single. If 'Heart Of Stone' occupied AOR territory and 'Young Hearts' was closer to emerging pop rock bands like T'Pau, then 'Let's Get Wet' was aimed squarely at the late 1980s pop market, with a busy, heavily synthesised production from Steve Glen. Bucks Fizz performed this song during their autumn 1988 live shows, at which point the song was a solo number for Shelley. Maybe it is because I first experienced the track in a live setting, but for me, 'Let's Get Wet' has always felt like Shelley's song, and I would like to have seen her retain the lead vocal with the song given a funkier band sound, closer in style to the live version. On streaming sites, this track is listed as a demo. It is also worth comparing it with Steve Glen's own version of the track on his album *The Shape Of Things To Come.*

The following track appeared on *The Best Of The Lost Masters & More!*:

'Young Hearts (Alternate Mix)' (Andy Hill)
A variation on the 2006 'Unreleased Version' that first appeared on *The Lost Masters,* with Cheryl on lead vocals, Bobby and Mike higher up in the mix during the verses and different ad-libs from Cheryl and Shelley over the chorus at the end.

Appendix 1 – OBF And The Fizz

The story of Bucks Fizz, OBF and The Fizz is a long, messy and convoluted one that requires a lengthy, descriptive chapter in some other book, but for the purposes of this section, I will be brief. 'Bucks Fizz' is a trademark (number 1162030) that was first registered by Big Note Music Limited in 1981. The current trademark (number 2137010) is owned by Heidi Manton, who joined Bucks Fizz in 1993 and is the wife of Bobby G. Only Bobby G's lineup is legally allowed to call themselves Bucks Fizz, and consequently, Cheryl Baker, Mike Nolan and Jay Aston have performed and recorded under the name OBF and later The Fizz.

Fame & Fortune? (2012)
Personnel
Mike Nolan: lead vocals, backing vocals.
Cheryl Baker: lead vocals, backing vocals.
Jay Aston: lead vocals, backing vocals.
Steve Stroud: bass, guitars, keyboards, accordion
Clive Carroll: guitars
Paul Hirsh: guitars, keyboards
David Colquhoun: guitars
Gary Clarke: keyboards
Peter May: drums, percussion
Melvin Duffy: steel guitar
Nik Carter: saxophone, horns
Jack Birchwood: trumpet, horns
Mark Kenevan: backing vocals on 'Joy!'
Producer: Steve Stroud
Engineer: Gary Clark
Executive producer: David Hahn
Sleeve design: Modo
UK release date: June 2012
Charts: did not chart
Track listing: 1. 'My Camera Never Lies', 2. 'Leave Them Alone', 3. 'Heart Of Stone', 4. 'This Day Is Mine', 5. 'I Hear Talk', 6. 'Joy!', 7. 'Can't Stand The Heat', 8. 'My Angel', 9. 'Talking In Your Sleep', 10. 'Love To Love', 11. 'Making Your Mind Up', 12. 'Ain't It A Shame (Ballad Of Bucks Fizz)'
An album of six original songs and six Bucks Fizz hits radically reimagined. Having flirted with reggae rhythms on tracks such as 'London Town' and 'If You Can't Stand The Heat', OBF just go for it on 'Leave Them Alone'. It works better than you might imagine, with Pete May and Steve Stroud holding down a solid rhythm, Mike Nolan's vocals front and centre and Nik Carter providing a fine sax solo. Jay Aston's 'This Day Is Mine', cowritten with Luc Floriani and Jay's partner David Colquhoun, is probably the strongest original track, a song about owning the day with all its possibilities and pitfalls and embracing

whatever it brings. 'My Angel' features a lovely solo vocal by Cheryl, tastefully augmented by Jack Birchwood's trumpet solo. Closing track 'Ain't It A Shame (Ballad Of Bucks Fizz)' is a country-style song, with sad, reflective lyrics that tell the story of the group. 'Can't Stand The Heat' has a full-on Spanish flavour to it, complete with an impressive flamenco-style guitar solo by Clive Carroll and Mariachi trumpets. Several of the reinterpretations have a leisurely jazz feel to them, including 'My Camera Never Lies', 'I Hear Talk' and, believe it or not, 'Making Your Mind Up'. Whisper it quietly, but I think I prefer this version.

The album was originally made available via the group's website. In 2014, OBF rebranded as 'Cheryl, Mike and Jay – Formerly of Bucks Fizz' and gained a temporary fourth member in Stephen Fox. In 2015, the group embarked on an extensive tour of the UK with Bobby McVay, former vocalist of 1983 Eurovision Song Contest entrants Sweet Dreams, as a permanent member of the lineup. *Fame And Fortune?* was subsequently reissued on vinyl in 2016 in a gatefold sleeve with Bobby McVay included on the cover. The album also included a CD and a black and white photograph.

The Fizz – The F-Z Of Pop (2017)

Personnel:
Cheryl Baker: lead vocals, backing vocals
Mike Nolan: lead vocals, backing vocals
Jay Aston: lead vocals, backing vocals
Bobby McVay: lead vocals, backing vocals
The Fizzy Gang on 'Up For The Fight' – Julian Bendle, Martin Blofeld, Julie Forsyth, Andrew Hodgskin, Chris Newbold, Paul Sillence, Lara Smith, Ian Stocker, Gill Trowbridge, Mark Wood, Tasha Worth
Dave Colquhoun: guitar on 'Where I'm Gonna Be' and 'Home For My Heart'
Recorded at MPG Studios, Surrey, between 2016 and 2017
Production and all other instrumentation: Mike Stock and Jimmy Junior
Mixed by Big Eared Boys except for 'The Land Of Make Believe 2017' mixed by Maestro Dave Ford
Photography: Claire Dominic
Artistic director: Jay Aston
Front cover design: Phil Gardner
Artwork and layout: Kate Stretton
UK release date: September 2017
Charts: UK: 25
Track listing: 1. 'Up For The Fight', 2. 'Break The Ice', 3. 'Where I'm Gonna Be', 4. 'Home For My Heart', 5. 'Dancing In The Rain', 6. 'Control Freak', 7. 'There's No Turning Back', 8. 'Amen', 9. 'My Camera Never Lies 2017', 10. 'Piece Of The Action 2017', 11. 'Land Of Make Believe 2017' 12. 'Up For The Fight (Extended Version)' 13. 'Break The Ice (Extended Version)' 14. 'Piece Of The Action 2017 (Extended Version)' 15. 'My Camera Never Lies 2017 (Karaoke)'
The vinyl version has additional track 'I Am The Beat'

This album saw Cheryl, Mike and Jay, now with Bobby McVay, rebrand themselves as 'The Fizz' and team up with writer and producer Mike Stock. The album came about initially by chance after Cheryl Baker and Mike Stock contacted each other via social media, following a suggestion by Andrew Hodgskin.

In Mike Stock, the group had someone with a gift for writing and producing strong commercial pop songs, and *The F-Z Of Pop* is crammed full of them. Lead single 'Dancing In The Rain' was the ideal introduction to the forthcoming album, a catchy pop song, with Bobby McVay on lead vocals alongside Mike, and those much-missed Fizz harmonies.

The album also gave the group a greater creative input; Mike Nolan and Bobby McVay wrote 'There's No Turning Back' with Mike Stock, Jay and Dave Colquhoun collaborated with him on 'Home For My Heart', which was later reworked and released as the album's third single, and Cheryl's daughter, Kyla Stroud, wrote, what is for me, the best track on the album, 'Amen', which became the album's second single. Quite how Cheryl didn't burst with pride every time she sang this song, I really don't know. Jay designed the album cover – a reference to the Sex Pistols and to the idea of the group being puppets – whilst a vinyl version had a psychedelic gatefold sleeve and featured an exclusive track, a cover of The Look's 'I Am The Beat'.

Personally, I loved this album. It was great to hear new music from Cheryl, Mike and Jay again, and as a Eurovision geek who remembered Bobby McVay from his time with Sweet Dreams (and later Dreams – yes, I bought their follow-up single, '17 Electric'), it felt like renewing an acquaintance. The four promotional videos that accompanied the singles were an added bonus, and on top of all that, the album charted, reaching number 25 in the UK.

Christmas With The Fizz (2018)

Personnel:
Cheryl Baker: lead vocals, backing vocals
Mike Nolan: lead vocals, backing vocals
Jay Aston: lead vocals, backing vocals
Bobby McVay: lead vocals and backing vocals ('Home For My Heart' and 'The Land Of Make Believe' only)
English Chamber Choir: vocals on 'Home For My Heart'
Dave Colquhoun: guitar on 'Don't Start Without Me', 'Home For My Heart' and 'Don't Start Without Me (Extended)'
Chris Lyndon: guitar on 'Winter Wonderland'
Rick Wakeman: piano on 'Home For My Heart'
Recorded at MPG Studios, Surrey, in 2018
Production and all other instrumentation: Mike Stock and Jimmy Junior
Mixed by Big Eared Boys except 'The Land Of Make Believe' mixed by Mix Maestro Dave Ford
Engineers: Chris Lyndon, except for 'The Land Of Make Believe' engineered by

Matt Parisi
Photography: Joseph Sinclair
Artistic director: Jay Aston
Design: Jay Aston, Phil Gardner, MPG
Artwork and layout: MPG
UK release date: November 2018
Charts: UK: 93
Track Listing: 1. 'Don't Start Without Me', 2. 'I Believe In Father Christmas', 3. 'Keeping The Dream Alive', 4. 'Mull Of Kintyre', 5. 'So Christmas', 6. 'Home For My Heart (Festive Mix)', 7. 'Wonderful Christmas Time', 8. 'Winter Wonderland', 9. 'Let It Snow, Let It Snow, Let It Snow', 10. 'Santa Claus Is Coming To Town', 11. 'What A Wonderful World', 12. 'White Christmas', 13 'River', 14. 'The Land Of Make Believe (Christmas Version)', 15. 'Don't Start Without Me (Extended Mix)'

Following the departure of Bobby McVay in early 2018, The Fizz were once again back to a trio of Cheryl, Mike and Jay. During the recording of this album, Jay Aston was diagnosed with cancer and had to have 40% of her tongue removed. Surgeons rebuilt Jay's tongue using tissue from her thigh, which was fed into her mouth through her neck. Faced with a very real possibility that she might not be able to sing or even speak again following these procedures, Jay recorded her vocal parts before undergoing treatment. Thankfully, the operation was a success, and Jay is now cancer-free. On the album credits, there is a special thank you from Mike and Cheryl to Guys Hospital, 'For giving us our Jay back. We are eternally in your debt.'

Mike Stock and Johan Kalel produced a fine original Christmas song, 'Don't Start Without Me', which kick-started the album. It was the lead single and featured a video of The Fizz on a steam train with Fizz fans making up their fellow passengers. My personal favourite on the album, though, is another Kyla Stroud song, 'So Christmas'. It is two and a half minutes of festive fabulousness: a fine lead vocal by Cheryl, wonderful supporting harmonies and a great song with a happy melody and evocative lyrics. What's not to love?

Cheryl pours her heart into a cover of Joni Mitchell's 'River' and does Joni and her beautiful, heartbreaking song credit. A 'Festive Mix' of 'Home For My Heart' is another album highlight; this version was adapted from the original on *The F-Z Of Pop* and had previously been released as a single. It is a suitably heartwarming track, and if you are looking for another connection between The Fizz and progressive rock, Rick Wakeman plays piano on this version and appears in the video.

In an article on *Broadway World* at the time of the album's release, Jay is quoted as saying, 'This has been a very unusual time for me with my health issues developing during the recording of the album. I am happy to report that things are much better now. We are so happy with the album, and we hope you agree. Merry Christmas, everyone ... now I realise every day is like Christmas.' Amen to that.

Smoke And Mirrors (2020)

Personnel:
Cheryl Baker: lead vocals, backing vocals
Mike Nolan: lead vocals, backing vocals
Jay Aston: lead vocals, backing vocals
Mike Stock and Jimmy Junior: keyboards, bass, guitars and programming
Dave Colquhoun: guitar solo on 'Winning Ways' and 'All We Ever Can Do'
The Westgroove Ensemble: brass and strings
Recorded at MPG Studios, Surrey, between June 2018 and September 2019
Producer: Mike Stock and Jimmy Junior
Mixed by Big Eared Boys
Engineer: Chris Lyndon
Photography: Joseph Sinclair
Grooming: Marcus Gurgel
Artistic director: Jay Aston
Design and layout: MPG
UK release date: March 2020
Charts: UK: 29
Track Listing: 1. 'Winning Ways', 2. 'All We Ever Can Do', 3. 'T.O.T.P', 4. 'From Here To Eternity', 5. 'More Than These Words', 6. 'Reservation', 7. 'The World We Left Behind', 8. 'Nothing's Gonna Last Forever', 9. 'Second To None', 10. 'Storm', 11. 'Boomerang'

Smoke And Mirrors was preceded by two singles. 'Winning Ways' was unveiled in January 2020, and it is a bit of a tough love song, directed towards someone wallowing in self-pity and complaining about how hopeless everything is. The lyrics encourage them to face the situation and 'Get back to winning ways'. It is another strong, commercial track with a quirky, humorous promotional video. The second single, 'T.O.T.P', was released in February. I loved the video, which was a laugh-out-loud homage to *Top Of The Pops* in the 1980s, but I was initially less sure about the song itself. It is infuriatingly catchy, though, and one of those songs that you will go around singing, whether you like it or not! Eventually, it wore me down, or I got over my initial misgivings, and I rather like it now.

'From Here To Eternity' was another single, and originally a dance track from 2001 by Natalie Browne, but The Fizz version transforms the song into a ballad that is the emotional heart of the album. Jay was recording her guide vocal for this track on the day she received her cancer diagnosis. She is outstanding on this track, delivering a powerful and moving lead vocal. Jay was unable to speak following her operation, so, to raise awareness, the video features signing from Isabella Signs, a YouTube star who learnt sign language in order to communicate with her younger brother Lucas, who has Down syndrome. I have my own personal connection to this song, too. At the time of the album's release, the UK was going into a COVID lockdown, and at the same time, my Mum was entering the advanced stages of dementia. I was her sole carer. 'From Here To Eternity' for me is about being there for someone you love with all of your heart, when they are confused and frightened, when they no longer know you, even though you know you will lose them, and it breaks your heart on a daily basis.

For me, several of the best tracks on the album were not singles. 'More Than These Words' has a Beatle-esque vibe to it, a timeless melody that you feel like you already know and a huge anthemic chorus. 'Storm' is superb with a definite *Tango In The Night* era Fleetwood Mac sound and is only edged out as my favourite track by 'Second To None', a fantastic pop/country crossover with a glorious hookline. 'The World We Left Behind' is another great track, and I saw the promotional video, which featured performance footage of The Fizz cut with scenes of Bucks Fizz winning the Eurovision in 1981, shortly after my Mum passed away in 2021. I remembered watching that same Eurovision with her, and this is a song that I can't listen to now without crying, as much out of love as sadness. Mike's song on the album, 'Nothing's Gonna Last For Ever', was also part of the healing process in the months that followed, reminding me to live in the moment, and this song, too, makes me tear up if the mood catches me. You see, it is not just disposable pop music.

Smoke And Mirrors gave The Fizz another top 40 album, reaching number 29 on the UK album charts. Discounting streaming and looking only at physical copies sold, it peaked at number six, the highest position of any album by either Bucks Fizz or The Fizz.

Everything Under The Sun (2022)

Personnel
Cheryl Baker: lead vocals, backing vocals
Mike Nolan: lead vocals, backing vocals
Jay Aston: lead vocals, backing vocals
Mike Stock and Jimmy Junior: keyboards, bass, guitars and programming
Josh Phillips: keyboards
Dave Colquhoun: guitar, keyboards
Chris Lyndon: programming
John Fordham: saxophone
Recorded at MPG Studios, Surrey
Producers: Mike Stock and Jimmy Junior
Mixed by Mixmaster Dave Ford
Engineer: Chris Lyndon
Photography: Simon Fowler
Styling: Jay Aston
Artwork and sleeve design: Jay Aston and MPG
Hair and makeup: Alison Butler
UK release date: September 2022
Chart: did not chart

Track listing: 1. 'I Wonder Where You Are Right Now', 2. 'Everything We Do (We Do It For You)', 3. 'A True Heart', 4. 'When Is Our Luck Gonna Change', 5. 'I Close My Eyes', 6. 'Treasure Forever', 7. 'You Can Find It Here', 8. 'Pretty Soon', 9. 'I'm On My Way (Better Run)', 10. 'This One'

With The Fizz celebrating 40 years together with a show at the Indig02, *Everything Under The Sun* seemed to be an album aimed squarely at their fans, with the album only available on CD, vinyl and digital download via the group's website. The album saw Mike Stock reunited with 'Mixmaster' Dave Ford, who mixed this album. The result is a record drenched in 1980s nostalgia, utilising a plethora of keyboards and technology from that period. Mike Stock produced a full list of these on his website, but they included Roland JX8P, Roland D-50, Roland U20, Roland Juno 60, Emulator II, Yamaha DX7, Korg M1, Korg DW 8000 and Mini Moog keyboards and the Linn 9000, Linn Drum, Roland 707 and Roland 727 drum machines. If you can imagine a Stock Aitken Waterman-produced Bucks Fizz album from the late 1980s, this is how it might have sounded.

It is fun noticing the references to other 1980s tracks, beginning with echoes of Don Henley's 'The Boys Of Summer' at the start of 'Everything We Do (We Do It For You)'. Queen fans may recall a Brian May hit from 1991 called 'Driven By You', which was initially written for a Ford commercial. 'Everything We Do (We Do It For You)' was written by Mike Stock and Pete Waterman in the early 1990s for the same promotional campaign, but was repurposed for The Fizz, as Mike Stock explains on his website:

> The brief for the original Ford commercial, for which it was intended, asked us to pay homage to all the Ford owners who, over the years, had remained faithful to the brand. At the time, Ford were not launching a new model, but they wanted an advert which kept everyone interested and showed Ford's love and respect for their customers. Of course, we didn't get the gig – Brian May did – but in thinking about The Fizz and 40 years as a brand, I remembered the track and thought with a bit of tinkering it could work well as The Fizz thanking their long-standing supporters.

'True Heart' incorporates another 1980s reference (I'm hearing 'Human' by Human League) with lyrics that reflect the bond between the group members and the way they have stood by each other in times of difficulty. 'I Close My Eyes' begins with the words 'It's easy to reminisce/'Bout a wonderful night like this/You'd think it was yesterday/But it's truly a life away'. Mike Stock indicates that the song refers to The Fizz remembering the night of their famous Eurovision victory in 1981. On his website, Mike Stock says these memories and feelings 'all happen inside their heads and recalls Eurovision 1981.' It is a lovely song, but the lyrics are not tied to a specific time and place and so can be applied to any fond reminiscence of a special time.

My favourite track on the album is the acoustic ballad 'Pretty Soon', a beautiful song with a tender lead vocal by Cheryl that is genuinely consoling and uplifting. Close behind it is 'I'm On My Way (Better Run)' with lead vocals by Mike, excellent harmonies on the chorus and references to several Bucks Fizz songs cleverly worked into the lyrics by Cheryl's daughter, Kyla. There were no promotional videos for this album, but there were a couple of TV appearances for 'This One' and 'Treasure Forever', which both went to number one on *The Heritage Chart*. I even memorised the routine to the latter in case The Fizz performed it at Wolverhampton Pride in 2023 before the heavens opened and intervened. Another year, maybe, he said hopefully!

Nothing lasts forever, but it would be nice to think that there is at least one more album collaboration between The Fizz and Mike Stock. If there isn't, then *Everything Under The Sun* gives this story a happy ending.

Appendix 2 – Compilations, Live Albums And Video Releases

Compilations

Few bands have had as many compilation albums issued as Bucks Fizz, with over 30 different collections released over the years. A fine place to start would be *The Land Of Make Believe – The Definitive Collection* (2023), a 5CD set with disc one presenting all 20 of the group's hit singles, with the original single mixes, properly remastered and in chronological order. The compilation also includes all of the 7" B-sides and a third disc of original extended remixes. Discs four and five offer something for hardcore Fizz fanatics with a disc of instrumental backing tracks and a disc of previously unreleased and seemingly newly created extended remixes, comprised of five singles and six flip sides or album tracks. For the less discerning Bucks Fizz fan, *The Very Best Of Bucks Fizz* (2007) is a good introduction. It doesn't include all the hits (it omits 'Rules Of The Game' and 'Magical'), but it contains the biggest ones. Some of the mixes are 'dead end' versions, however, rather than the original single versions. Some copies contain a DVD featuring the group's promotional videos, which is their only officially sanctioned release in that format.

If you can find them, then *The Lost Masters* (2006) and *Lost Masters 2 – The Final Cut* (2008) are essential purchases. These double CDs are a treasure trove of previously unreleased extended mixes, alternate versions, demos, unreleased tracks and solo material. Many of these tracks have since appeared on the 2015 Definitive Editions of the group's albums, but by no means all. Some of the tracks were replicated on the digital album *The Best Of The Lost Masters And More!* (2013) and the 2CD *Remixes And Rarities* (2014), each of which features previously unreleased material alongside newly created remixes.

Sony BMG have issued a number of compilations that are worth seeking out. *The Ultimate Anthology* (2005) is a 2CD set featuring all of the group's hit singles, though again not all of the original mixes. It does benefit from a second CD of extended versions that includes the 12" mix of Cheryl's solo single 'If Paradise Is Half As Nice' and the corresponding B-side 'This Fragile Heart'. The 3CD *Legends* (2005) is a 42-track mixed bag of singles, album tracks and B-sides originally released by RCA in random order. Far better is the 4CD *The Platinum Collection,* which provides a space for more obscure tracks such as 'Every Dream Has Broken', 'I Used To Love The Radio' and the Bobby G solo track 'Alibi' in addition to a new acoustic mix of 'Heart Of Stone'. *Up Until Now ... (The 30th Anniversary Hits Collection)* (2011) was released to coincide with the 30th anniversary of the group's formation and Eurovision victory. The title is a little misleading as 'When We Were Young', 'London Town' and 'Rules Of The Game' are all TV mixes, 'You And Your Heart So Blue' is a 2011 remix and 'Heart Of Stone' features Cheryl on lead vocals. If you are looking for a compilation of the group's hit singles in the form that they were originally released, then this is probably not the collection for you. However, these alternate versions, some of them exclusive to this release, along with newly created extended remixes of 'Magical' and 'What's Love Got To Do With It' on disc two, make it a worthwhile purchase for Bucks Fizz completists.

There were two vinyl Bucks Fizz albums released in North America. The first of these, *Bucks Fizz* (RCA Victor NFL1-8029) (1982), is different to the album of the same name released in the rest of the world and features a unique sleeve. Side one contains the same track listing as *Are You Ready,* but with 'One Of Those Nights' replacing the title track. Side two replaces 'Another Night' with 'Piece Of The Action' and moves 'Land Of Make Believe' to the opening song. A second album, *New Beginning* (Polydor 422-831 096-1 Y-1) (1986), was a ten-track compilation of songs from *Are You Ready, Hand Cut, Greatest Hits, I Hear Talk* and *Writing On The Wall.*

There have been numerous budget compilations over the years, beginning with Camden's ten-track vinyl *Making Your Mind Up* in 1983, Music For Pleasure's *The Land Of Make Believe* in 1986 and Pickwick's *Golden Days* (1992). The latter was the first CD appearance for several tracks, including 'Where The Ending Starts' and 'I Hear Talk', long before any CD reissue of their parent albums.

By the late 1990s, there were two versions of Bucks Fizz in existence, one featuring Bobby G and another group featuring David Van Day and Mike Nolan. This resulted in a compilation of rerecorded Bucks Fizz songs by the latter, sometimes billed as *The Very Best Of Bucks Fizz* (1996) but reissued eight times with the same tracks in various guises. These CDs feature three new songs written by this lineup: 'Let's Party (All Night)', '(Gimme One More) Chance' and 'Lazy With Your Love'. It is good to hear Mike's voice, but these recordings are cheap-sounding and, curiosity value aside, I would recommend seeking out the vastly superior originals instead.

Live Albums

Bucks Fizz only issued one live album: *Live At The Fairfield Hall, Croydon*. It was recorded in September 1990 and released the following year to coincide with the group's tenth anniversary. Following the departure of Shelley Preston at the end of 1989, Bucks Fizz were down to a trio of Bobby G, Cheryl Baker and Mike Nolan. Several of the musicians featured had been part of the group's touring band during the 1980s, including Alan Coates (guitar and vocals), Steve Stroud (bass and vocals) and Tom Marshall (keyboards and vocals). The album was the group's first and only release on Jet Records (JETLP 1001). As Electric Light Orchestra (who were, and still are, my favourite band) and local rock legend Ozzy Osbourne also released albums on Jet Records in the late 1970s and early 1980s, this made me happier than you might imagine. The 13-track album features Bucks Fizz hit singles alongside late 1980s chart hits, including 'We Built This City' and 'You're The

Voice'. The album was also released on CD and cassette and reissued in 1992 with a new title, *The Best Of & The Rest Of Bucks Fizz Live* (Action Replay Records) and *The Best And The Rest* (Merlin Records). Both versions omitted 'Groovy Kind Of Love' from this release. The concert was also broadcast on BBC Radio 2 on 21 March 1992. In 2012, *Writing On The Wall – The Ultimate Edition* included a 'Motown Medley' and a 'Rolling Stones Medley' that were recorded at the same show.

The Fizz have also self-released a live CD, *Fizzion 2020,* recorded at the EM Forster Theatre, Tonbridge, on 17 October 2020. Alongside Bucks Fizz hits, it featured selected tracks from *The F-Z Of Pop* and *Smoke And Mirrors,* and it was also available as a DVD.

El Mundo De Ilusion

Track listing: 1. 'Otra Noche (Another Night)', 2. 'Hoy Siento Soledades (Getting Kind Of Lonely)', 3. 'Via Libre (One Way Love)', 4. 'Brillar (Shine On)', 5. 'Todo Ha Terminado (Now You're Gone)', 6. 'El Mundo De Ilusion (The Land Of Make Believe)', 7. 'Yo Se Que Es Amor (It's Got To Be Love)', 8. 'Robos Y Asaltos (Breaking And Entering)', 9. 'Eso Fue Ayer (Now Those Days Are Gone)', 10. 'Noches Sin Ti (One Of Those Nights)'

In 1982, Bucks Fizz released an album exclusively for the Latin American market with ten tracks recorded in Spanish. The Spanish lyrics were written by Buddy McCluskey (real name Howard Dean McCluskey), an Argentinian singer and composer who was working for RCA at that time, and his wife, Mary McCluskey. Together, they had composed the lyrics for ABBA's Spanish album *Gracias Por La Música,* which boosted the group's popularity in Spanish-speaking countries. The Bucks Fizz album was released in Argentina, Chile and Bolivia, but one of the singles taken from it, 'Yo Se Que Es Amor', had an even wider reach with releases in Spain, Mexico, Argentina, the Philippines, Chile, El Salvador and Peru.

The album is not simply the existing backing tracks with Spanish lyrics sung over the top, as several of the tracks have notable differences from their English language counterparts. For example, 'Eso Fue Ayer (Now Those Days Are Gone)' features piano at the start of the second verse and the final verse is sung by the whole group and not just Mike. The classical guitar solo on 'Yo Se Que Es Amor (It's Got To Be Love)' continues into the final chorus. 'Via Libre (One Way Love)' features electric guitar chords instead of the harmonies at the start of the track and the song fades out early; 'Robos Y Asaltos' omits the sound effects present at the start of 'Breaking And Entering'; 'El Mundo De Ilusion (The Land Of Make Believe)' fades out without the poem spoken at the end; and 'Hoy Siento Soledades' features a longer instrumental section at the end than its English language version, 'Getting Kinda Lonely'. This release also enabled the group to promote the album in South America. Just prior to the release of *Hand Cut,* the group performed in Chile on 13 and 14 February 1983 at Festival Internacional de la Canción de Viña del Mar, which was broadcast in Chile, selected South American countries and Spain. Both of their live sets included 'Noches Sin Ti' and 'El Mundo De Ilusion'.

Five of these songs were included as a bonus on the 2004 CD reissue of *Bucks Fizz,* and the full album finally received a UK release in 2015 when it formed all of disc two on *Bucks Fizz: The Definitive Edition*. It is certainly a lot easier than obtaining a vinyl copy by mail order from Argentina in the pre-internet 1980s.

Video Releases

The first Bucks Fizz release was a VHS Video in 1986, *Greatest Hits: Less Bucks More Fizz,* which featured all of the group's promotional videos, starting with 'You And Your Heart So Blue' and working backwards chronologically. A second VHS release of promotional videos, *The Best Of Bucks Fizz,* was available by mail order only from Razzmatazz Management in 1992. The only official DVD release of any of the group's promotional videos came as part of the 2007 compilation *The Very Best Of Bucks Fizz.*

In 2010, *The Bucks Fizz Story* was released as a limited-edition DVD. The DVD is out of print now, but it is a very honest documentary and well worth tracking down. A 2DVD Special Edition was also available, containing bonus live and interview footage and a video of OBF's 'I Hear Talk'.

None of the group's concert tours from the 1980s received an official release, but thanks to some brilliant work from the multi-talented Stephen Fox, unofficial DVDs of the group's 1983 Christmas Shows at the London Apollo, 1984 Tour and 1985 *Magical Tour* were created. None of these were originally filmed with a view to a commercial release, and all the footage is from one camera, but they are all entertaining and keep the full shows intact. These DVDs sold out very quickly, but they are worth looking out for, especially if you attended one of the shows on these tours.

The Fizz have been much more active with several self-published concert DVD releases, including *All That Glitters* (2012), *35th Anniversary Show* (2016) and *Fizzion 2020* (2020) available via their website.

Appendix 3 – Pre Bucks Fizz: Brooks, Co Co And The Main Event

Prior to joining Bucks Fizz, Mike Nolan was in a group called Brooks, who released six singles. In 1975, Cheryl Baker joined a band called Mother's Pride, who subsequently became Co Co and briefly The Main Event. I thought it might be helpful to have a little overview of these releases for those who would like to explore the group's history and the records Mike and Cheryl were involved with before Bucks Fizz.

Brooks Singles

'Sound Of Our Love' (D.M.A Loewenthal) b/w **'Showdown'** (Peter Pereira) (1979)

'Cry (Till My Eyes Run Dry)' (L. Steymel) b/w **'One Love, One Heart'** (Peter Pereira) (1979)

'What A Great Night For Makin' Love' (Barry Mason/Roger Greenaway) b/w **'Now Or Never'** (Peter Pereira) (1979)

'What A Great Night For Falling In Love' (Barry Mason/Roger Greenaway) b/w **'Now Or Never'** (Peter Pereira) (1979)

'Don't You Know A Lady (When You See One)?' (Mike Leander/Roger Greenaway) b/w **'One Night Stand'** (Peter Pereira) (1980)

'We Are United' (A. Arthurs/Roger Greenaway) b/w **'Jenny Is A Girl Of Many Parts'** (Peter Pereira) (1980)

Brooks were put together in 1976 by Freya Miller, at which point their lineup consisted of Mike Nolan, Peter Pereira, Ricky Galahad and Chris Hamill (also known as Limahl). The group's first single, 'The Sound of Your Love', featured Peter Pereira on lead vocal, by which time, John Humphreys had replaced Chris Hamill. Mike Nolan assumed lead vocal duties for the next few singles, and Roger Greenaway took over as producer and co-writer for the group's final single of 1979, the disco-themed pop song 'What A Great Night For Makin' Love' (Polydor POSP 88). Unfortunately, the title was deemed a bit too racy for the BBC, and so the single was reworked as 'What a Great Night For Falling In Love' (Polydor POSP 98) and reissued in a picture sleeve.

There were two further singles in 1980: 'Don't You Know A Lady (When You See One)?', which had previously been recorded by Brian Connolly, former lead vocalist with The Sweet, and 'We Are United', which featured John Humphreys on lead vocal. By this stage, Ben Ellison had replaced Ricky Gallahad, and although the group continued to promote themselves with television appearances and magazine features, a chart hit had continued to prove elusive, and the group went their separate ways shortly afterwards. Excerpts of TV clips featuring Brooks appeared in The Bucks Fizz Story DVD, and a clip of the group performing the Queen song 'Seaside Rendezvous' from a *Dick Emery Thames TV Special* can be found online and on DVD.

Co Co

'Wake Up' (David Hayes/Phil Dennys) (Alan Merrill/Jake Hooker) b/w **'Love Love'** (Phil Dennys) (1976)

Prior to Cheryl joining Mother's Pride in 1975, the group had released two singles on Pye Records: 'Follow The Man With The Music' b/w 'Time After Time' (released in January 1975) and 'Oh Well, Oh Well' b/w 'Little Debbie' (released May 1975). By 1976, the group had changed their name to Co Co, and 'Wake Up' was not only their first release under their new name (and the first to feature Cheryl) but also an entry for the 1976 Song For Europe.

The contest was held at the Royal Albert Hall on 25 February 1976. 'Wake Up' was the first of 12 songs competing, and it led for most of the voting, only slipping into second place in the penultimate round and finishing two points behind the eventual winners Brotherhood Of Man with 'Save Your Kisses For Me'. The single was released in a picture sleeve in the UK and was also issued in Portugal, Spain and Japan, each of which had a unique picture sleeve. Although the song was credited on the night and on the record to David Hayes and the group's producer Phil Dennys, it emerged years later that much of it was written by Alan Merrill and Jake Hooker of the group Arrows, who also wrote the classic 'I Love Rock N Roll'. In an interview with Carl Wiser on the website songfacts.com, Alan Merrill explains:

> I came up with a song called 'Wake Up', which was almost The Arrows' second single. Mickie (Most) didn't think it was any good. To show how discerning he was, David Hayes changed the lyrics and put it out with Co Co in 1976, two years after we presented it to Mickie, and it almost won Eurovision (sic). Came in number two, by Co Co. Exactly the same melody, same arrangement, same chorus, only Dave changed some of the lyrics. My name is nowhere on the credits. Ours is in 1974, theirs is in 1976. We were clearly first, and that's the dirty music business.

The Arrows' previously unreleased version of 'Wake Up' can be heard on their *A's, B's, And Rarities* compilation from 2004.

'Don't Push Me Round' (Terry Bradford/Keith Hasler/Peter Pereira) b/w **'You Know What It's Like'** (Terry Bradford) (1976)

The group's first self-penned single and the last to feature Peter Pereira, who departed the group shortly afterwards to form Brooks.

'Money Song' (Terry Bradford/Nat Kipner) b/w **'Save Me'** (Kipner/Vallius/James) (1977)

A new lineup for Co Co, with the addition of Paul Rogers and Josie Andrews. 'Money Song' is a jolly, quirky little tune that picked up airplay in Europe but was not a chart success for the group in the UK. There was no picture sleeve for the UK issue, but there was a lovely one for releases in Germany, the Netherlands and Italy.

'Bad Old Days' (Stephanie De Sykes/Stuart Slater) b/w **'Get You Out Of My Life'** (Terry Bradford/Nat Kipner) (1978)

Having turned down the chance to perform 'Promises Promises' in the 1977 contest, and with an album already recorded and finished, Co Co were offered 'Bad Old Days'. The song was initially written with Demis Roussos in mind as a slow, plaintive number, although co-writer Stephanie De Sykes remarked, 'we beefed it up for the contest.' Co Co's arrangement changed the song and the performance of it, but when *A* Song For Europe was held at the Royal Albert Hall on 31 March 1978, Co Co, augmented by drummer Charlie Brennan, swept to victory, finishing 19 points clear of their nearest rival.

'Bad Old Days' became Co Co's only hit, reaching number 13. The group performed the song on *Miss England* 1978 on 5 April (one of the contestants was a 17-year-old Jay Aston, who was 'Miss Purley') and made two appearances on *Top Of The Pops* on 6 April 1978 (Episode 740) and again on 20 April 1978 (Episode 742), which was repeated on 4 May. Other performances included *Pebble Mill At One* on 12 April 1978, *The Val Doonican Show* on 15 April 1978, *Cheggers Plays Pop* on 17 April 1978 and a charming promotional clip shot near Tower Bridge in London for the Eurovision Song Contest Previews show on 16 April 1978. Co Co represented the United Kingdom at the 1978 Eurovision Song Contest at the Palais des Congres in Paris on 22 April 1978. The song received a total of 61 points and finished 11th.

Bad Old Days (1978)

Track listing: 1. 'Bad Old Days', 2. 'I Can't Talk Love On The Telephone Line', 3. 'Ain't No Point In Buying Oysters', 4. 'Money Song', 5. 'How Can I Make It Baby On My Own', 6. 'Keep Singing Those Love Songs', 7. 'Jamboree Band', 8. 'California Here I Am', 9. 'Get You Out Of My Life', 10. 'Comme Ci Comme Ca', 11. 'Keep Moving', 12. 'Silhouette'

Bad Old Days was the only album by Co Co. 'How Can I Make It Baby On My Own' was covered the following year by Johnny Mathis with a slightly amended title and featured on his top 40 album *The Best Days Of My Life*. Also worth seeking out for Fizz fans is 'Comme Ci Comme Ca', which features a lead vocal from Cheryl. The album cover for most territories was a close-up shot of the group in their 'Bad Old Days' clown make-up, but the Japanese and Australian versions each have different sleeves.

'I Can't Talk Love On The Telephone Line' (Terry Bradford/Nat Kipner) b/w **'Take A Look At My Baby'** (Terry Bradford/Nat Kipner) (1978)

'Way Out' (Terry Bradford) b/w **'Don't You Worry 'Bout Me'** (Terry Bradford) (1978)

'I Can't Talk Love On The Telephone Line' is a pretty acoustic ballad lifted from the album and paired with a new track on the flip side. The group's final single of 1978 consisted of two new songs: 'Way Out' moved the group a little more towards a pop-rock style, whilst 'Don't You Worry 'Bout Me' was a ballad featuring only Terry Bradford on vocals.

'Harry My Honolulu Lover' (Terry Bradford) (Demo) (1979)
A song written by Terry Bradford for the 1979 Song For Europe. The song is a throwback to the dance band era of the early 1930s (to my ears, it sounds like a Foxtrot) and was given to The Nolan Sisters. Anne Nolan is the lead vocalist on their version and the sisters styled it with their close harmony vocals and developed a cute and visually appealing routine to go along with it. Unfortunately, a strike by the Association of Broadcasting Staff meant that the 1979 Song For Europe was cancelled, with the songs judged purely on their recorded versions. The Nolan Sisters' version finished fourth in the contest, and it was released as a single in 1979. Cheryl Baker sang on the demo of the track, having been asked to do so as a favour to Terry Bradford. The promotional video of the Nolan Sisters performing the song can be found on their official YouTube channel. Another clip of them performing it on *The Val Doonican Show* on 21 April 1979 gives an indication of how the song would have been staged in the Song For Europe, and the original demo with Cheryl's vocals can also be found online.

'Keep On Dancing' (Graham Sacher) b/w **'One Side Of A Triangle'** (Terry Bradford) (1980)
Co Co's final single appears to have been released only in Germany on RCA Records. Unusually, production duties were relinquished to Graham Sacher, who produced both sides of the single. The A-side was a happy little song in a similar style to Tony Christie's 'Ladies Man' (also written and produced by Graham Sacher and released in 1980), which harked back to an easy listening style of a couple of years earlier. The B-side, 'One Side Of A Triangle', is of interest to Bucks Fizz fans as it features a lead vocal from Cheryl that only appears on this single.

The Main Event
'Gonna Do My Best' (Terry Bradford) b/w **'When Your Mama Takes Ya Home'** (Terry Bradford) (1980)
Effectively Co Co's swan song, 'Gonna Do My Best' was one of 12 songs in the 1980 Song For Europe, held on 26 March 1980 at the BBC Television Theatre in Shepherd's Bush. The Main Event was Terry Bradford, Keith Hasler, Cheryl Baker and Helen Baley, although Josie Andrews and Julie Roberts appeared with them onstage for the live performance. It was a pleasant song, though not a likely winner, and finished in 12th place with 45 points.

Appendix 4 – Solo Material

Bobby and Cheryl released solo singles under their own names in the 1980s; however, solo material, released from 2006 onwards, can often be found on Bucks Fizz compilations or as part of *The Lost Masters* series. Additionally, Mike, Cheryl and Jay have also released their own albums. I have attempted to bring these solo tracks together in one place, put them in chronological order and add a little bit of context where possible.

Bobby G

'Big Deal' (Bobby G) b/w **'It's All For Jan'** (Bobby G) (1984)
In 1984, Bobby wrote and produced the theme for the BBC drama *Big Deal,* a highly enjoyable series that ran from 1984 to 1986 starring Ray Brooks as Robbie Box, a likeable but flawed gambler who is always looking for that one big deal, and Sharon Duce as his long-suffering girlfriend Jan Oliver, hence the song title of the flip side. Buoyed by the popularity of the show, the single became a hit, reaching number 46 in the UK but staying on the charts for 12 weeks. The song was incorporated into the group's live set as a solo number for Bobby during the *Magical Tour* in 1985.

Related Tracks
'Big Deal (Extended Version)' (Bobby G)
'Alibi' (Bobby G)
Both of these tracks were on the original 12" single of 'Big Deal'. The extended mix later appeared on *The Best Of The Lost Masters & More!* whilst 'It's All For Jan' and 'Alibi' (a solid track which would have made a really good Bucks Fizz B-side) featured on 2009's *The Platinum Collection*.

'Technicoloured Love Affair' (Bobby G) (Unreleased) (1985)
Dramarama was a children's TV series that was broadcast between 1983 and 1989. The shows were 30-minute stand-alone dramas, often with a supernatural, science fiction or satirical theme. The finale of season three, broadcast in July 1985, was entitled 'Purple Passion Video'. Written by Matthew Bardsley, the show starred Bobby G as 'Kid', Suzannah Grant as 'Girl' and Michael O'Hagan as Kid's controlling minder. It is a surreal story about two young fans wanting to meet Kid and appear in one of his videos, with a twist at the end that reveals that all is not as it appears. Bobby provided the music for the episode, and this track plays over the opening and end credits and appears at intervals throughout the story.

'Big Deal' (Bobby G) b/w **'I Want To Stay'** (Bobby G) (1986)
With Bucks Fizz signing a new record deal with Polydor in 1986 and *Big Deal* in its third and final series, the track was remixed by Bobby G and Brian Tench and reissued on Polydor Records in a new picture sleeve. Sadly, it was not a hit on this occasion.

Related Tracks
'Big Deal (1986 Extended Version)' (Bobby G)
'I Want To Stay (Unedited Version)' (Bobby G)
The 1986 reworking of 'Big Deal' also had an extended version that was released on a 12" single. The 7" and 12" versions and a previously unreleased, unedited version of the B-side 'I Want To Stay' were included on *Writing On the Wall – The Ultimate Edition*.

Although Bobby released no further solo material, several tracks recorded between 1984 and 1988 appeared on later Bucks Fizz albums. The following two songs featured on *The Lost Masters:*

'I Can't Live Without Love (1986 Version)' (Mary Unobsky/Daniel Ironstone/David Harvey)
'I Can't Live Without Love (1987 Version)' (Mary Unobsky/Daniel Ironstone/David Harvey)
A rock power ballad with a sing-along chorus that is perfectly suited to Bobby's voice. The 1986 version was produced by Bobby with Trevor Vallis, while Bobby produced the later version alone, although it seems a little redundant, as the 1986 version got it right the first time. Swedish singer Tove Naess also recorded the track; it featured on her 1987 album *Shine On* and was released as a single in her native country.

The following two tracks appeared on *The Lost Masters 2 – The Final Cut*:

'Putting The Heat On' (Bobby G)
'Because Of Susan' (Bobby G)
'Because Of Susan' is an alternate version of the previously released 'It's All For Jan', but with a different vocal and lyric, which would place it circa 1984. 'Putting The Heat On' is an up-tempo track that would appear to date from the same period.

These three tracks appeared on *Writing On The Wall – Ultimate Edition*:

'One Heart' (Steve Glen/Mike Burns/Bobby G)
'I Should Have Been Strong' (Steve Glen/Mike Burns/Bobby G)
'Innocent' (Steve Glen/Mike Burns/Bobby G)
All of these songs date from 1988 and were produced by Steve Glen. 'One Heart' is an AOR ballad with a memorable hook line that Bucks Fizz could have recorded. 'I Should Have Been Strong' is curious as Bobby adopts an affected vocal, a little reminiscent of Michael McDonald in places, whilst 'Innocent' has shades of Richard Marx. Perhaps these are attempts to explore different styles, but they create the impression of being written with a view to other artists recording them.

Cheryl Baker

'If Paradise Is Half As Nice' (Lucio Battisti/Jack Fisman) b/w **'This Fragile Heart'** (Andy Hill) (1987)

Cheryl's debut solo single, produced by Andy Hill. The A-side had previously been a UK number one hit for Amen Corner in 1969. The 12" featured an extended version, and both the 7" and 12" were backed by the sensitive 'This Fragile Heart', which I actually preferred to the A-side. Sadly, the single stalled outside the top 75, peaking at number 94. Both the extended version and 'This Fragile Heart' can be found on *The Ultimate Anthology*. Later that summer, Cheryl appeared on the game show *321,* where she performed 'If You're Right', an early Hill/Sinfield composition first recorded by Lulu in 1981. In a brief conversation with the host, Ted Rogers, Cheryl indicated that she was recording a solo album: 'I'm working on an album now. It hasn't got a title yet, but I'm looking forward to finishing it.' The album never materialised, unfortunately, but several tracks recorded around that period appeared on *The Lost Masters:*

'If Paradise Is Half As Nice (Original Version)' (Lucio Battisti/Jack Fisman)
'What's One Lonely Woman' (Andy Hill/Don Black)
'Skin On Skin' (Andy Hill)
'If You're Right (Original Version)' (Andy Hill/Pete Sinfield)
'If You're Right (Re-Recorded Version)'

Andy Hill produced all of the above tracks. The rerecorded version of 'If You're Right' dates from 1987 but was unfinished. It was subsequently mixed and completed by Dean Murphy in 2006.

The following track, dating from 1988, appeared on *Writing On The Wall – Ultimate Edition*:

'Easy Trouble' (Steve Glen/Mike Burns)

A fine pop song over a backing track that became the Dollar hit 'It's Nature's Way (No Problem)'. Given that Steve Glen co-wrote and produced tracks with Bobby and Shelley around this period, it is not clear whether these tracks were conceived as solo songs, demos for other artists or potential material for the group.

'Sensuality' (Barry/Torch) b/w **'Love To Love'** (Stroud/Parks/Stroud) (1992)

Billed simply as 'Cheryl', this chilled-out electronic dance track was released as a stand-alone single in 1992. There was a 7" Radio Mix, a 12" Club Mix that could be found on the CD and cassette singles, too, plus an 'Ultra Sensual' mix on the 12" Promo. It was written by Steve Torch, who later co-wrote

'Everything I Wanted' for Dannii Minogue and Pandora's 'On A Night Like This', which became a massive hit for Kylie Minogue, and Paul Barry, whose credits include hit songs by Tracie and Delta Goodrem. They both contributed to writing Cher's iconic hit, 'Believe'.

Cheryl Sings Joni (2017)

Track listing: 1. 'Free Man In Paris', 2. 'Big Yellow Taxi', 3. 'Chinese Café', 4. 'Both Sides Now', 5. 'Carey', 6. 'Chelsea Morning 17', 7. 'People's Parties', 8. 'California', 9. 'A Case Of You', 10. 'Chelsea Morning', 11. 'Raised On Robbery', 12. 'Help Me'

A self-released album that was preceded by an EP of the first four songs in a different card sleeve entitled *Cheryl Sings Joni – Part 1*. All lead and female backing vocals were by Cheryl, with Jamie Moses providing the rest and Steve Stroud playing fretless bass on 'Chinese Café'.

Mike Nolan

In My Life (2013)

Track listing: 1. 'Desperado', 2. 'Can't Take My Eyes Off You', 3. 'Alone Again (Naturally)', 4. 'Elusive Butterfly', 5. 'I Made It Through The Rain', 6. 'Never Let Her Slip Away', 7. 'Everything I Own', 8. 'Everlasting Love', 9. 'When You Were Sweet Sixteen', 10. 'Stuck In The Middle With You', 11. 'You've Got A Friend', 12. 'Wichita Lineman', 13. 'You Got It', 14. 'In My Life'

The first of Mike's self-published albums, which he describes in the sleeve notes as 'the most poignant album of my career.' It is a collection of the songs that helped Mike regain his memory following the coach crash in Newcastle in 1984 and helped to give him the strength to fight back and continue performing.

Rose Of Cimarron (2016)

Track listing: 1. 'Girls Talk', 2. 'Ruby, Don't Take Your Love To Town', 3. 'Arms Of Mary', 4. 'Take It Easy', 5. 'Sundown', 6. 'Islands In The Stream', 7. 'Love Hurts', 8. 'Rhinestone Cowboy', 9. 'Annie's Song', 10. 'Walk Of Life', 11. 'The Most Beautiful Girl', 12. 'Rose Of Cimarron'

An enjoyable country-themed album that benefits from a fine collection of songs well-suited to Mike's voice. 'Islands In The Stream' is a duet with Cheryl Baker, whilst the title track was included as a solo spot for Mike during The Fizz's concerts at the time of the album's release.

Time On My Side (2024)

Track listing: 1. 'Eight Days A Week', 2. 'Just When I Needed You Most', 3. 'Time On My Side', 4. 'When You Walk In The Room', 5. 'Amazed', 6. 'Raincloud', 7. 'You Needed Me', 8. 'Rhythm Of The Rain', 9. 'Blue Bayou', 10. 'First Of May (2000)'

Another self-published collection that coincided with Mike stepping down from The Fizz. It is great to hear Mike's rendition of 'Rhythm Of The Rain', a UK one-hit wonder by The Cascades that my dad introduced me to.

Jay Aston

Shape Up And Dance (1984)

Track listing: 1. 'Living A Life Of Love', 2. 'It's Only Love', 3. 'I Do It All For You', 4. 'Piece Of The Action', 5. 'Theme From 'Flashdance' – What A Feeling', 6. 'She Works Hard For The Money', 7. 'Every Breath You Take', 8. 'If You Can't Stand The Heat (Get Out Of The Kitchen)', 9. 'Alright', 10. 'We Might Fall In Love'

The seventh in the series of exercise and fitness albums that were popular in the early 1980s. Jay was an ideal choice to record such an album, not only as a member of Bucks Fizz but as someone who had taught fitness and dance. The music on these albums is almost secondary and serves as an accompaniment to the fitness instructions, but Jay livens up her album by turning 'Living A Life Of Love' (originally recorded by Zinc) into a kind of English Will Powers, complete with motivational self-talk and a humorous cast of characters. Jay promoted the album in an interview with Tommy Boyd on *Saturday Starship,* and vinyl copies came with an eight-page instruction booklet.

Alive And Well (2002)

Track listing: 1. 'Pigs Are On The Cake', 2. 'Stay With Me', 3. 'Waiting For The Day', 4. 'Jack 'N' Jill', 5. 'Wednesday's Child', 6. 'Sorrows Wedding', 7. 'Everlasting Love', 8. 'Yours Truly', 9. 'Love, Hate & Gasoline', 10. 'Objects Of Desire', 11. 'Rosie Banks', 12. 'Lox', 13. '13', 14. 'Everlasting Love (Dance Mix)'

If you have heard Bucks Fizz and think you know what a Jay Aston solo album might sound like, I strongly advise you to throw those preconceptions in the bin. From the angst-ridden 'Sorrow's Wedding' to the feel-good vibes of 'Everlasting Love', the perfect pop of 'Yours Truly', the haunting 'Jack N Jill', via driving rock ('Rosie Banks'), electronic dance (the psychologically intense 'Lox'), roots rock and grunge ('Pigs Are On The Cake'), *Alive And Well* is a surprising and wildly eclectic album. Jay wrote a track-by-track commentary on her website at the time, and several of these tracks are deeply personal. The album sounds nothing like Bucks Fizz, but it is a rewarding listen. In 2011, Jay appeared as Claudia Brite in the film *The Last Days Of Edgar Harding,* written and directed by Stephen Fox. A video to 'Rosie Banks', which features in the soundtrack, was posted online to promote the DVD release of the film in 2013.

Lamb Or Lizard (2006)

Track listing: 1. 'Robot Romeo', 2. 'There's No Other Place', 3. 'Lovin' You', 4. 'Wednesday's Child', 5. 'In Your Eyes', 6. 'Heaven's Ransom', 7. 'Lost And Lonely', 8. 'River Of Light', 9. 'Free Falling', 10. 'Sanctuary', 11. 'As U Like It', 12. 'Pray', 13. 'Suffocating Cindy', 14. 'Mr X', 15. 'King Of Pain', 16. 'Regarding This Notoriety', 17. 'Feel To Heal', 18. 'Bohemian Love', 19. 'Emotional Graffiti', 20. 'Cryptic King', 21. 'The Salt Of Plenty', 22. 'Human Lace', 23. 'Ice Cold Was Alice', 24. 'Wish I Was Here', 25. 'Naked Phoenix', 26. 'Lamb & Lizard', 27. 'Blackness Lane', 28. 'Wire Sun', 29. 'Serial Killer', 30. 'Love, Hate & Gasoline', 31. 'Moon And Sun', 32.

'The Unknown Gunman', 33. 'Tongue', 34. 'Here Comes The Judge', 35. 'Justify My Love', 36. 'Stay', 37. 'I'm Coming Home', 38. 'Hell Of A Lullaby', 39. 'Suffocating Cindy (Guitar Version), 40. 'Disorder At The Dream Shrine', 41. 'Wicked Ways', 42. 'Baby Sledgehammer', 43. 'Blue Day', 44. 'Candy Man', 45. 'Show Me Love', 46. 'I'm Coming Back'

The original cassette version of *Lamb Or Lizard* was made available via mail order in September 1993, with an accompanying photo album available separately. In 2006, Jay delighted her fans by issuing an expanded 3CD edition exclusively via her website, effectively turning it into an anthology of her solo work. Initial copies of the 3CD album were signed and contained 46 songs, including two tracks recorded in 1979: 'Robot Romeo' and 'There's No Other Place'. These were removed from later copies, which contained 44 tracks and featured a reworded and slightly amended sleeve design. The digital version of the album currently found on streaming sites features 37 tracks, including one song, 'Butterflies', not found on the CD versions.

I Spy (2016)

Track listing: 1. 'The Insecure Chief', 2. 'True Love', 3. 'Music Box', 4. 'The Law Of Happiness', 5. 'Great Expectations', 6. 'Fundamental Flaw', 7. 'Sometimes', 8. 'The God Song', 9. 'The Fool', 10. 'Stay With Me (Acoustic)'

'True Love' was the lead single and has a bit of a Lily Allen vibe, complete with a promotional video that doesn't take itself too seriously. 'True Love' was issued as a one-track promotional CD single, as was 'Great Expectations', a powerful ballad that Jay performed during The Fizz shows. Also worth seeking out is the DVD *Jay Aston In Concert With Truth Is,* a one-off show filmed at The Barn Theatre, Oxted, in March 2017. Here, Jay is backed by her songwriting partner (and husband), Dave Colquhoun, and his band, Truth Is. The concert, which has since been uploaded to Jay's official YouTube channel, features all but two of the tracks from *I Spy* and selected songs from Jay's extensive back catalogue. Look out, too, for Jay's friend, the fabulous Denise Waterman (of Tight Fit), on backing vocals.

Zenshoppers

'Sorrows Wedding'/'Morphine'/'Unknown Song' (1997)

In between the cassette release of *Lamb Or Lizard* and *Alive And Well* came a one-off CD single by Jay and Dave Colquhoun on the Industrial/dance label Pandemonium Records (PANNCD15) under the name Zenshoppers. 'Unknown Song' was not listed as such but had an unpronounceable title consisting of a string of emojis.

Shelley Preston

These three tracks appeared on *The Lost Masters*:

'I Love Music (Edit)' (Kenneth Gamble/Leon Huff)

'These Boots Are Made For Walking' (Lee Hazelwood)
'Move Over (I'm Driving)' (Andy Hill)
'I Love Music' was a cover of the O'Jays track produced by Simon Harris in 1987; an extended 'Dream Mix' later appeared on streaming sites. 'These Boots Are Made For Walking' was also recorded in 1987 with Pete Woodroofe producing, but remained unfinished. Shelley's vocals were rerecorded in November 2005, and the song was mixed and completed by Dean Murphy the following year. 'Move Over (I'm Driving)' is an original track written by Andy Hill that features both Shelley and Cheryl. It is a fresh, fun pop song that would be released under the Bucks Fizz name on this album, but it is so different from the type of material Andy Hill was writing for the group that it doesn't sound like it was composed with the group in mind. By the mid-1980s, many of the songs Andy Hill was writing for Bucks Fizz had a thoughtful and broadly rock-oriented/AOR slant: 'You And Your Heart So Blue', 'Keep Each Other Warm', 'I Hear Talk', 'Heart Of Stone', 'Every Dream Has Broken'. 'Move Over (I'm Driving)' is nothing like that; it is an upbeat, keyboard-driven dance pop song with an empowering lyric. It would have been a great track for Bucks Fizz to release in the late 1980s, although it would have been atypical of their material at that time, and the absence of Mike or Bobby on this track makes me wonder whether it was intended as a solo track for Shelley or a contender for Cheryl's solo album instead. Shelley rerecorded her vocals in November 2005, and the song was mixed and finished by Dean Murphy that year. There are two cover versions of this song, both by Paul Chiten, one featuring Sue Sheridan and a later one with Suzi Quatro on Paul Chiten's 2017 album *Songz 8*.

The following track featured on *Writing On The Wall – Ultimate Edition*:

'Paper Hearts' (Steve Glen/Mike Burns)
One of several tracks produced by Steve Glen that were recorded with individual members of the group in 1988. This dance-oriented track has something of a pop/soul feel to it.

2Deep (1991)
'Life Party (Tribal Mix)'
'Surrender (Sex Mix)'
'Life Party (Tribal 7")'
'Surrender (Interlude)'
'Surrender (Love Mix)'
'Life Party' is a euphoric early 1990s dance track written and produced by drummer Chris Blackwell for a Reebok TV commercial called 'The Edge'. He played all the instruments himself, and Shelley was the featured vocalist. All versions of 'Surrender' are remixes and variations of 'Life Party' with a different song title.

Cloudfish (2006)

Track listing: 1. So High, 2. My Space, 3. The Kiss, 4. Letting Go, 5. Leap Of Faith
After Spandau Ballet went their separate ways in the early 1990s, saxophonist Steve Norman moved to Ibiza and worked on projects with a number of people, including music producer and DJ Rafa Peletey, who was based there. They formed a 'chillout' band, Cloudfish, which included Shelley as vocalist. This mini-album was released in the summer of 2006.

Backing Vocals And Related Work

As a massive fan of the band Queen, I saw Brian May on tour a couple of times in 1993, and I was delighted to see Shelley as part of his touring band. Shelley can be heard and seen on The Brian May Band's *Live At The Brixton Academy* CD and video. It is also worth seeking out the televised performance from the Barcelona date on this tour as it features Shelley prominently during 'Love Token', which was heavily edited in the official video. Shelley also featured on the live material that was included on the reissue of *Back To The Light* and on Brian's 1998 album *Another World,* where she provided backing vocals for the studio versions of 'On My Way Up' and 'All The Way From Memphis'.

After leaving Bucks Fizz at the end of 1989, Shelley could often be seen on television or on tour with artists including Jason Donovan, INXS (Shelley can be seen briefly in their video for 'Searching'), Michael Bolton, Go West, Beverley Craven (Shelley also provided backing vocals on selected tracks for her 1993 album *Love Scenes*), Gary Moore, Alison Moyet, Alexander O'Neal, Belinda Carlisle, Westlife, Guns 'N' Roses, Paul Young, Tony Hadley, Donny Osmond, Curtis Stigers and Luther Vandross. Live appearances by Shelley, including some of her original material and collaborations, can be found online.

Appendix 5 – Odds And Ends And Later Remixes

Odds And Ends

'Laughter Show Theme' (Bobby G)

The Laughter Show was a BBC comedy sketch show, starring Les Dennis and Dustin Gee, that premiered in 1984. Bobby G wrote and sang the theme music for this show. A recording of the theme (lasting for 43 seconds) is an uncredited bonus track on disc one of *Lost Masters 2.* This version is different to the one used for the show itself as it features Andy Hill on backing vocals instead of Cheryl Baker.

'Happy Christmas From The Stars'

Bucks Fizz featured on this double-sided flexi disc given away with *Smash Hits* issue 9-22 December 1982. The magazine described it as 'bristling with Christmas greetings from 44 famous pop stars and cunningly crammed with all manner of festive sound effects.'

'B.I.N.G.O' (Unreleased)

In 1982, Bucks Fizz sang and appeared in a short commercial to promote a bingo competition for the *News Of The World* newspaper. The jingle used the melody of the 1980 Ottawan hit 'D.I.S.C.O' but changed the lyrics to become 'B.I.N.G.O/Play News Of The World Bingo'.

The Assistants – 'Down At The Superstore' (B.A. Robertson/Alec and Pearl) (1982)

Saturday Superstore was a British children's television series that was shown on BBC 1 and ran from October 1982 to April 1987. This was the theme tune to the show, produced and co-written by B.A. Robertson, who was also a member of 'The Assistants' along with Cheryl Baker, Junior, Suzi Quatro and Dave Edmunds. It was released as a single in 1982 (BBC Records and Tapes RESL 122), and a promotional video was made to accompany it.

Who Cares – 'Doctor In Distress' (Ian Levine/Fiachra) (1985)

A well-intentioned but ill-advised charity single released to call for a reprieve for the popular BBC TV show *Dr Who,* which at that time had been suspended and appeared to be facing cancellation. The Bucks Fizz connection to this record is Bobby G, who appears alongside series regulars Colin Baker (the sixth Doctor) and Nicola Bryant (the Doctor's companion, Peri Brown), among other musicians and performers.

People In Progress – 'This Is My Song' (Leee John/Ashley Ingram) (1986)

A much better charity record written by Leee John and Ashley Ingram of the band Imagination. It was recorded in July 1986 to raise money for Sickle Cell Anaemia Relief and the Canon Collins Educational Trust for Southern Africa. Mike Nolan featured among the chorus.

Ferry Aid – 'Let It Be' (Paul McCartney/John Lennon) (1987)
On 6 March 1987, the ferry MS Herald of Free Enterprise capsized, killing 193 passengers and crew. All proceeds from sales of this single, which was a UK number one, were donated to the charity set up in the aftermath of the Zeebrugge disaster. Bucks Fizz are credited as part of the chorus, and Shelley can be seen several times in the accompanying video, with Mike appearing briefly in the background.

Later Remixes

There have been a number of official remixes of Bucks Fizz songs, especially over the last 20 years. Some of these completely redesign the track around the vocals, others are contemporary-sounding mixes constructed from the source material and a few contain newly recorded vocal parts. Rather than commenting on each one, which would require a much bigger book, here is a list of these newly created mixes and where to find them.

Bucks Fizz The Definitive Edition

'One Of Those Nights (2012 Extended Version)'
'Piece Of The Action (Stephen Vadin Dedication Mix)'
'Making Your Mind Up (Original Fat Dog Remix)'
'Making Your Mind Up (2011 Anniversary Remix)'
'Making Your Mind Up (Matt Pop's Bending The Rules Mix)'

Are You Ready The Definitive Edition

'The Land Of Make Believe (1991 Chris Paul Remix)'
'The Land Of Make Believe (1991 Dance Funk Remix)'
'The Land Of Make Believe (2008 Extended Version)'
'My Camera Never Lies (2006 'Good Eyes' Remix)'
'My Camera Never Lies (2014 7" Remix)'
'My Camera Never Lies (2014 Extended Remix)'
'My Camera Never Lies (2014 Ross Alexander Remix Radio Edit)'
'Now Those Days Are Gone (2006)'
'Easy Love (2014 Extended Remix)'

Hand Cut The Definitive Edition

'Run For Your Life (2008 Extended Version)'
'Running Out Of Time (Extended Version)'
'When We Were At War (2012 Extended Remix)'
'Oh Suzanne (Cheryl Vs Jay)'

The Lost Masters 2 – The Final Cut

'Magical (The Rock Mix)'
'Golden Days (2008 Extended Version)'
'Every Dream Has Broken (Sugar Cube Vs Bucks Fizz 2007 Remix)'

The Best Of The Lost Masters And More! (Digital Only)
'Every Dream Has Broken (2010 Extended Version)'
'Heart of Stone (Cheryl Lead Extended Version)'
'I Hear Talk (Extra Talk Mix)'
'One Of Those Nights (2012 7" Mix)'
'Every Dream Has Broken (Original Sugar Cube Remix)'
'Making Your Mind Up (A Cappella)'

The Ultimate Anthology
'My Camera Never Lies (1987 Remix)'

Writing On The Wall – The Ultimate Edition (2012)
'Soul Motion (2011 Extended Version)'

Remixes And Rarities
'Young Hearts (2013 Remix)'

The Platinum Collection
'Heart Of Stone (2009 Acoustic Version)'

Up Until Now – The 30th Anniversary Hits Collection
'Heart Of Stone (2011 Cheryl Baker Lead Vocal)'
'You And Your Heart So Blue (2011 Mix)'
'What's Love Got To Do With It (Extended Version)'
'Magical (Extended Version)'

The Land Of Make Believe – The Definitive Collection
'Making Your Mind Up (Extended)'
'Took It To The Limit (Extended)'
'The Land Of Make Believe (1991 Dance Funk Remix-Extended Version)'
'If You Can't Stand The Heat (Alternate Extended Mix)'
'January's Gone (Extended Mix)'
'In Your Eyes (Extended Mix)'
'Too Hard (Extended Mix)'
'I Need Your Love (Extended Mix)'
'Don't Turn Back (Extended Mix)'
'New Beginning (Dub Funk Extended Version)'
'Love The One You're With (Dub Funk Extended Version)'

There is also a remix of the previously unreleased Cheryl Baker track 'What's One Lonely Woman (Laid Back Mix 2011)' on *Writing On The Wall – The Ultimate Edition*.

Bibliography

Although much of this book came from my own knowledge, scrapbooks, cassettes and record collection, there were some excellent resources that proved invaluable. These websites were:

discogs.com
imdb.com
nostalgicmusictv.x10host.com
songfacts.com
totparchive.co.uk
tvpopdiaries.co.uk
andrewggibson.com
secondhandsongs.com
mikestockmusic.com

And the following books were used for quotes and referencing:

Garfield, S., *Expensive Habits* (Faber and Faber, 1986)
Marshall, T., *Catch A Falling Star* (Self-Published, 2023)
Nash, G., *Wild Tales* (Penguin, 2013)
Roxbugh, G., *Songs For Europe Volume Two: The 1970s* (Telos Publishing, 2014)
Roxbugh, G., *Songs For Europe Volume Three: The 1980s* (Telos Publishing, 2016)

On Track series

AC/DC – Chris Sutton 978-1-78952-307-2
Allman Brothers Band – Andrew Wild 978-1-78952-252-5
Tori Amos – Lisa Torem 978-1-78952-142-9
Aphex Twin – Beau Waddell 978-1-78952-267-9
Asia – Peter Braidis 978-1-78952-099-6
Badfinger – Robert Day-Webb 978-1-878952-176-4
Barclay James Harvest – Keith and Monica Domone 978-1-78952-067-5
Beck – Arthur Lizie 978-1-78952-258-7
The Beat, General Public, Fine Young Cannibals – Steve Parry 978-1-78952-274-7
The Beatles 1962-1996 – Alberto Bravin and Andrew Wild 978-1-78952-355-3
The Beatles Solo 1969-1980 – Andrew Wild 978-1-78952-030-9
Blue Oyster Cult – Jacob Holm-Lupo 978-1-78952-007-1
Blur – Matt Bishop 978-178952-164-1
Marc Bolan and T.Rex – Peter Gallagher 978-1-78952-124-5
David Bowie 1964 to 1982 – Carl Ewens 978-1-78952-324-9
David Bowie 1963 to 2016 – Don Klees 978-1-78952-351-5
Kate Bush – Bill Thomas 978-1-78952-097-2
The Byrds – Andy McArthur 978-1-78952-280-8
Camel – Hamish Kuzminski 978-1-78952-040-8
Captain Beefheart – Opher Goodwin 978-1-78952-235-8
Caravan – Andy Boot 978-1-78952-127-6
Cardiacs – Eric Benac 978-1-78952-131-3
Wendy Carlos – Mark Marrington 978-1-78952-331-7
The Carpenters – Paul Tornbohm 978-1-78952-301-0
Nick Cave and The Bad Seeds – Dominic Sanderson 978-1-78952-240-2
Eric Clapton Solo – Andrew Wild 978-1-78952-141-2
The Clash (revised edition) – Nick Assirati 978-1-78952-325-6
Elvis Costello and The Attractions – Georg Purvis 978-1-78952-129-0
Crosby, Stills and Nash – Andrew Wild 978-1-78952-039-2
Creedence Clearwater Revival – Tony Thompson 978-1-78952-237-2
Crowded House – Jon Magidsohn 978-1-78952-292-1
The Damned – Morgan Brown 978-1-78952-136-8
David Bowie 1964 to 1982 – Carl Ewens 978-1-78952-324-9
David Bowie 1964 to 1982 – Carl Ewens 978-1-78952-324-9
Deep Purple and Rainbow 1968-79 – Steve Pilkington 978-1-78952-002-6
Deep Purple from 1984 – Phil Kafcaloudes 978-1-78952-354-6
Depeche Mode – Brian J. Robb 978-1-78952-277-8
Dire Straits – Andrew Wild 978-1-78952-044-6
The Divine Comedy – Alan Draper 978-1-78952-308-9
The Doors – Tony Thompson 978-1-78952-137-5
Dream Theater – Jordan Blum 978-1-78952-050-7
Bob Dylan 1962-1970 – Opher Goodwin 978-1-78952-275-2
Eagles – John Van der Kiste 978-1-78952-260-0
Earth, Wind and Fire – Bud Wilkins 978-1-78952-272-3
Electric Light Orchestra – Barry Delve 978-1-78952-152-8
Emerson Lake and Palmer – Mike Goode 978-1-78952-000-2
Fairport Convention – Kevan Furbank 978-1-78952-051-4
Peter Gabriel – Graeme Scarfe 978-1-78952-138-2
Genesis – Stuart MacFarlane 978-1-78952-005-7
Gentle Giant – Gary Steel 978-1-78952-058-3
Gong – Kevan Furbank 978-1-78952-082-8
Green Day – William E. Spevack 978-1-78952-261-7
Steve Hackett – Geoffrey Feakes 978-1-78952-098-9
Hall and Oates – Ian Abrahams 978-1-78952-167-2
Peter Hammill – Richard Rees Jones 978-1-78952-163-4
Roy Harper – Opher Goodwin 978-1-78952-130-6
Hawkwind (new edition) – Duncan Harris 978-1-78952-290-7
Jimi Hendrix – Emma Stott 978-1-78952-175-7
The Hollies – Andrew Darlington 978-1-78952-159-7
Horslips – Richard James 978-1-78952-263-1
The Human League and The Sheffield Scene – Andrew Darlington 978-1-78952-186-3
Humble Pie –Robert Day-Webb 978-1-78952-2761
Ian Hunter – G. Mick Smith 978-1-78952-304-1
The Incredible String Band – Tim Moon 978-1-78952-107-8
INXS – Manny Grillo 978-1-78952-302-7
Iron Maiden – Steve Pilkington 978-1-78952-061-3
Joe Jackson – Richard James 978-1-78952-189-4
The Jam – Stan Jeffries 978-1-78952-299-0
Jefferson Airplane – Richard Butterworth 978-1-78952-143-6

Jethro Tull – Jordan Blum 978-1-78952-016-3
J. Geils Band – James Romag 978-1-78952-332-4
Elton John in the 1970s – Peter Kearns 978-1-78952-034-7
Billy Joel – Lisa Torem 978-1-78952-183-2
Journey – Doug Thornton 978-1-78952-337-9
Judas Priest – John Tucker 978-1-78952-018-7
Kansas – Kevin Cummings 978-1-78952-057-6
Killing Joke – Nic Ransome 978-1-78952-273-0
The Kinks – Martin Hutchinson 978-1-78952-172-6
Korn – Matt Karpe 978-1-78952-153-5
Led Zeppelin – Steve Pilkington 978-1-78952-151-1
Level 42 – Matt Philips 978-1-78952-102-3
Little Feat – Georg Purvis – 978-1-78952-168-9
Magnum – Matthew Taylor – 978-1-78952-286-0
Aimee Mann – Jez Rowden 978-1-78952-036-1
Ralph McTell – Paul O. Jenkins 978-1-78952-294-5
Metallica – Barry Wood 978-1-78952-269-3
Joni Mitchell – Peter Kearns 978-1-78952-081-1
The Moody Blues – Geoffrey Feakes 978-1-78952-042-2
Motorhead – Duncan Harris 978-1-78952-173-3
Nektar – Scott Meze – 978-1-78952-257-0
New Order – Dennis Remmer – 978-1-78952-249-5
Nightwish – Simon McMurdo – 978-1-78952-270-9
Nirvana – William E. Spevack 978-1-78952-318-8
Laura Nyro – Philip Ward 978-1-78952-182-5
Oasis – Andrew Rooney 978-1-78952-300-3
Phil Ochs – Opher Goodwin 978-1-78952-326-3
Mike Oldfield – Ryan Yard 978-1-78952-060-6
Opeth – Jordan Blum 978-1-78-952-166-5
Pearl Jam – Ben L. Connor 978-1-78952-188-7
Tom Petty – Richard James 978-1-78952-128-3
Pink Floyd – Richard Butterworth 978-1-78952-242-6
The Police – Pete Braidis 978-1-78952-158-0
Porcupine Tree (Revised Edition) – Nick Holmes 978-1-78952-346-1
Procol Harum – Scott Meze 978-1-78952-315-7
Queen – Andrew Wild 978-1-78952-003-3
Radiohead – William Allen 978-1-78952-149-8
Gerry Rafferty – John Van der Kiste 978-1-78952-349-2
Rancid – Paul Matts 978-1-78952-187-0
Lou Reed 1972-1986 – Ethan Roy 978-1-78952-283-9
Renaissance – David Detmer 978-1-78952-062-0
REO Speedwagon – Jim Romag 978-1-78952-262-4
The Rolling Stones 1963-80 – Steve Pilkington 978-1-78952-017-0
Linda Ronstadt 1969-1989 – Daryl O. Lawrence 987-1-78952-293-8
Roxy Music – Michael Kulikowski 978-1-78952-335-5
Rush 1973 to 1982 – Richard James 978-1-78952-338-6
Sensational Alex Harvey Band – Peter Gallagher 978-1-7952-289-1
The Small Faces and The Faces – Andrew Darlington 978-1-78952-316-4
The Smashing Pumpkins – Matt Karpe 978-1-7952-291-4
The Smiths and Morrissey – Tommy Gunnarsson 978-1-78952-140-5
Soft Machine – Scott Meze 978-1078952-271-6
Sparks 1969-1979 – Chris Sutton 978-1-78952-279-2
Spirit – Rev. Keith A. Gordon – 978-1-78952- 248-8
Stackridge – Alan Draper 978-1-78952-232-7
Status Quo the Frantic Four Years – Richard James 978-1-78952-160-3
Steely Dan – Jez Rowden 978-1-78952-043-9
The Stranglers – Martin Hutchinson 978-1-78952-323-2
Talk Talk – Gary Steel 978-1-78952-284-6
Talking Heads – David Starkey 978-178952-353-9
Tears For Fears – Paul Clark – 978-178952-238-9
Thin Lizzy – Graeme Stroud 978-1-78952-064-4
Tool – Matt Karpe 978-1-78952-234-1
Toto – Jacob Holm-Lupo 978-1-78952-019-4
U2 – Eoghan Lyng 978-1-78952-078-1
UFO – Richard James 978-1-78952-073-6
Ultravox – Brian J. Robb 978-1-78952-330-0
Van Der Graaf Generator – Dan Coffey 978-1-78952-031-6
Van Halen – Morgan Brown – 9781-78952-256-3
Suzanne Vega – Lisa Torem 978-1-78952-281-5
Jack White And The White Stripes – Ben L. Connor 978-1-78952-303-4
The Who – Geoffrey Feakes 978-1-78952-076-7
Roy Wood and the Move – James R Turner 978-1-78952-008-8
Yes (new edition) – Stephen Lambe 978-1-78952-282-2
Neil Young 1963 to 1970 – Opher Goodwin 978-1-78952-298-3
Frank Zappa 1966 to 1979 – Eric Benac 978-1-78952-033-0
Warren Zevon – Peter Gallagher 978-1-78952-170-2
The Zombies – Emma Stott 978-1-78952-297-6
10CC – Peter Kearns 978-1-78952-054-5

... and many more to come!